Knowledge Development Innovation: How To Rescue America's Advantage

Knowledge Development Innovation: How To Rescue America's Advantage

For Joan

Boultm

12/12/06

BOULTON B. MILLER PH.D.

To order additional copies of this book, contact:
Xlibris Corporation
1-888-795-4274
www.Xlibris.com
Orders@Xlibris.com
26010

Contents

To my friend and mentor Mohammad Dadashzadeh, Ph.D.

INTRODUCTION

OVER A DECADE ago, when I was employed as a full-time visiting professor in the School of Business Administration, College of William and Mary, I began working on the application of knowledge development in high schools, colleges, and universities. Although at the time there were those who believed "knowledge creation" was a better term than "knowledge development," I based my choice on the fact that knowledge builds on knowledge while creation is the development of new knowledge. Creation of knowledge is important in the field of education; however, in classrooms, students must build on previous knowledge they have acquired. The creation of new knowledge may begin in any classroom; however, it most often occurs in graduate schools or through specific research efforts.

I have written two other papers about knowledge development that are on my Web site, *http://boultonmiller.com*: "Knowledge Development: Raising Education and Training to a New Level" (1994) and "Knowledge Development Update" (1999). In the 1994 document, I recommended the formation of a **department of knowledge development** in place of the Departments of Labor and Education. This new department emphasizes the development of knowledge rather than wasting energy and resources to educate only half our people while the rest work.

I was never able to determine if my 1994 knowledge development report, referenced above, contributed toward the **1995 proposal** initiated in the House of Representatives for the merger of the two departments. Representative Steve Gunderson from Wisconsin drafted the 1995 proposal; however, he did not acknowledge receiving my report, nor did he return to Congress.

Such a proposal is not without historical precedent. In **England**, in 1995, the Departments for Education and Employment merged. These departments are similar to our Departments of Education and Labor. In January 2003, then-secretary of state for education and skills, Charles Clarke, presented a white paper to Parliament entitled "The Future of Higher Education." This paper points out the benefits of the British higher education system and the great assets it produces for both individuals and the nation. Their pride in their universities is well documented and includes recognition of the research capacity that is considered strong and, at best, world class. However, the paper indicates that there is no room for complacency due to the growing challenges from other countries. The paper also shows that their higher education system is under pressure and at risk of decline as budgets are tightened. Nowhere in the paper was any reference that the combined departments were anything but successful organized in the **Department of Education and Skills** (Clarke 2003).

The **white paper** stated that fewer than one in five businesses taps into universities' skills and knowledge; however, the paper did promise increased funding to provide a network of twenty knowledge exchanges to reward and support higher education institutions working with business.

Prior to recommending a department of knowledge development in 1994, I was influenced by the differences between **training** and **education**. The labor department appears to be oriented toward training for jobs, jobs, and more jobs, while the education department seems to be dominated with information technology, statistics, and grants. Both need the support of the unions to meet the new objectives of developing knowledge. All concerned need to support each other in changing American methods of education and training. This national effort will make a difference. There have been many discussions about training and education. In education, there is little training beyond the professions such as medicine and law as training is generally episodic and comprehensive, containing everything you need to know in order to perform a specific task. Education, on the other hand, like knowledge, is deeply imbedded in culture and about a beginning, not an end.

Vartan Gregorian believes that for most students, college is a time for self-discovery, for developing passionate interests, and for weaving these interests into a meaningful career. In 1999 the Mellon Group, a market-research consulting firm, surveyed college students younger than thirty-one years of age and found that 80 percent said it is "very important" for them to find work that "will make a positive difference in people's lives." Unfortunately, colleges have taken what he calls the "home depot" approach to education where colleges are becoming academic superstores, vast collections of courses, stacked like sinks and lumber for do-it-yourselfers to try to assemble a meaningful curriculum on their own. The fundamental problem underlying a disjointed curriculum is the fragmentation of knowledge itself. By dividing knowledge into disciplines, subdisciplines, and sub-subdisciplines, knowledge breaks into smaller unconnected fragments of academic specialization. This calls for a reform of higher education to reconstruct the unity and value of knowledge. This is complicated by the total amount of collected information doubling every two or three years. Many high schools do not do their jobs; 53 percent of college students, including those who attend community colleges, require remedial courses. In addition, almost 60 percent of the students attend two or more colleges, and many students have family or work responsibilities. College students spend less than half the time on their studies than the faculty expects. According to President Gregorian, the challenge for higher education is not the choice between pure research and practical application but, rather, the integration and synthesis of compartmentalized knowledge. On our campuses, we must create an intellectual climate that encourages faculty members and students to make connections among seemingly disparate disciplines, discoveries, events, and trends and to build bridges among them that benefit the understanding of us all (Gregorian 2004).

In addition to my recommendation for the new department of knowledge development, in the 1994 report, I proposed that a **knowledge development agency** be formed in a bipartisan effort similar to the Manhattan Project (for the development of the atomic bomb) or the National Aeronautics and Space Administration (NASA). Such a major effort is necessary to redirect the education of our students. This effort is more complicated today because in the past decade we have allowed the integration of computers to support most all of our activities, expanding our use of networks, and the development of new uses for the Internet at an alarming rate. The increase in the volumes of data being generated, and the information provided from these data, are major problems in need of solutions.

Note that the following section is included to emphasize the critical increases in the amount of data accumulating on a daily basis and to show some of the steps being taken to manage this increase.

DATA

FROM THE 2003 eleventh edition of *Merriam Webster's Collegiate Dictionary,* data are defined as "information in numerical form that can be digitally transmitted or processed" (Webster 2003a).

From the 2003 tenth edition of *Webster's New World Computer Dictionary,* data are defined as "factual information (such as text, numbers, sounds, and images) in a form that can be processed by a computer" (Webster 2003b).

William W. Agresti recalls the predictions in the 1970s of a great data famine with millions of computers fighting for the same small piece of data like savages. "Today, our data silos are overflowing. We find new ways to grind every human experience into finer and finer granularity. Business that once viewed transaction data as plumbing the depths of detail are now buried in click stream data, which for one company alone exceeds 250 GB (gigabyte) per day and is growing. NASA archives more than 1 TB (terabyte) of earth science data per day, while the National Institutes of Health database of genetic sequence information doubles every eighteen months. Coconspirators in the great data glut are the increasingly plentiful and cheap silos; worldwide digital data storage capacity doubles every nine months, while the cost per gigabyte of magnetic disk volume declined by a factor of five hundred from 1990 to 2000. With heaps of data growing exponentially, the task of mining it for relationships that might translate into new knowledge grows more daunting. We are 'informing ourselves to death,' consciously collecting more data than we need, with every good intention of figuring out later what really is worth saving. An attractive alternative preventive is to put filtering in the forefront, admitting only worthwhile data. But we do not always know in advance what really is worth collecting. Failing to grab data may be an irreversible decision, as I learned supporting NASA, where it's really important. We haven't found a way to realign heavenly bodies to give us a second chance at data capture" (Agresti 2003).

Data quality problems cost U.S. businesses an estimated $600 billion per year. Successful corporations have rigorous and defined quality assurance and improvement programs that help them build better products faster and cheaper. These techniques are used to eliminate or minimize defects during the production and maintenance of their products to meet customer expectations. But companies have not taken the same approach to improving the quality of their data production and maintenance (English 2004).

Although most often viewed from an economic point of view, there are enormous gains from **globalization**. Seldom do we find two books that are so similar in reminding us of the advantages of globalization. Jadish Bhagwan, a native of India but a tenured professor at Columbia University, and Martin Wolf, an assistant editor of London's *Financial Times* who spent many years as a World Bank economist, have both written books about globalization. Bhagwan's book is *In Defense of Globalization*, and Wolf's book is *Why Globalization Works*. Although not addressing the issue of data quality, both authors set the stage for recognition of the data problems as data are accumulated and consolidated in a global environment (Bartlett 2004).

The explosive increase in the amount of data created during the past decade has been and is receiving much needed attention. One example is Eliot Christian, of the U.S. Geological Survey, who initiated **GILS (Global Information Locator Service)**. GILS is required under U.S. law (44 USC 3511) and policy (OMB Memo 98-5) at the U.S. federal level and is cited in the laws and policies of various U.S. states and other nations. Christian stated in an e-mail that he understood that Brazil has begun nationwide implementation of GILS and that he was just back from Kuwait where he had been advising on their GILS implementation (Christian 2003).

The goal of **GILS** is to facilitate people finding the information needed. Every day there are mountains of data created by government, industry, and other institutions. Driven by warp-speed advances in computer and communications technology, the information creation rate accelerates. GILS is described as a revolutionary new approach designed to address one of the most crucial challenges we will face in the twenty-first century, enabling people to find and retrieve information easily even as information sources expand and diversify. Fundamentally, GILS is not about picking new information technologies but about managing information content.

GILS defines an open, low-cost, and scalable standard enabling governments, companies, or other organizations to help searchers find collections of information, as well as specific information in the collections. Large or small organizations can use GILS, whether they are technically advanced or just starting out. A researcher can describe anything from printed documents, to lists of experts, to complex data, using GILS. The Clearinghouse for Geospatial Data extends GILS to help searchers find map products and answer questions using the vast range of data referenced to places on the earth.

Anyone who has used a library can use **GILS** because it is based on the ISO 23950 search standard and includes the most commonly understood concepts by which people worldwide find information sources in libraries—concepts like title, author, publisher, data, and place. A GILS's locator record is an advanced version of the library catalog record. It is noted that technologies may come and go, but the content of information resources must not be lost in the shuffle. Use of the common search approach used by GILS allows us to leverage our treasure-houses of accumulated knowledge, exploit the full breadth of the Internet today—and position us for the future (GILS 2003).

Note that the discussion of GILS could have been included under a later heading, "Information"; however, the author considered that due to the importance of the volume of data, an earlier introduction was justified.

The **Federal Geographic Data Committee (FGDC)** is a nineteen-member interagency committee composed of representatives from the executive office of the president, cabinet level, and independent agencies. The FGDC is developing the **NSDI (National Spatial Data Infrastructure)** in cooperation with organizations from state, local, and tribal governments; the academic community; and the private sector. The NSDI encompasses policies, standards, and procedures for organizations to cooperatively produce and share geographic data (FGDC 2003).

In December 2002, the U.S. Congress approved the **National Digital Information Infrastructure and Preservation Program's (NDIIPP)** plan **Preserving Our Digital Heritage.** This plan would make it possible for the Library of Congress to proceed with the work of developing an infrastructure for the collection and preservation of digital material. NDIIPP is a nationwide initiative being led by the Library of Congress that has a strong interest in forming partnerships with a wide range of stakeholders as it works to develop a network of committed organizations and institutions (NDIIPP 2003).

In 1790, the U.S. Congress requested the **first official census** completed in 1792; and became the first nation in the world to make the census a mandatory constitutional requirement. An accurate breakdown of the population was needed to ensure that each state was assigned a fair number of congressional representatives. Every American household was visited by federal marshals, hired by Congress. At that time, six simple questions were used that included who was the head of the household, race, and gender. A census is completed every ten years, though surveys are now mailed instead of delivered by individuals on horseback. Although the questions have changed, the census remains a valuable research tool for historians, sociologists, economists, and scholars of all types. The **U.S. Census data** are the leading examples of how data have changed during the past decade.

The **U.S. Census collection** is the best tool for filling in the blank pages of your family history. You can search through more than 450 million names using every U.S. Federal Census from 1790 through 1930. Family facts like age, residence, occupation, and more are available. Up to six generations of your American heritage are available to search through more than 140 years of history (Census 2000).

A great improvement found in the 2000 census is the **easy access to facts** about people, business, and geography. For example, when Kansas was entered into the search field, almost two pages of data were displayed. Under the heading People QuickFacts, examples of the data included population; percent of change; percent of persons under five years, under eighteen years, those sixty-five years of age and older; percentage of high school graduates and those with bachelor's degree or higher, plus income by household, and per capita money income. Under Business QuickFacts, the data included the number of private nonfarm establishments, private nonfarm employment, and percent of minority-owned and women-owned firms. Under Geography QuickFacts, the land area was given in square miles and persons per square mile, and the same for United States of America. When Sedgwick County, Kansas was entered, similar data appeared under the same QuickFacts headings (QuickFacts 2000).

The 2000 census data is the foundation for the use of **census software** by TETRAD Computer Applications Inc. This makes it easy to profile locations and find target market areas anywhere in the United States. Profiling provides a complete demographic report for a geographic area that you describe using circles, polygons (neighborhoods or trade areas), or drive times. The data can also be displayed for standard census areas (states, counties, places, census tracts, or block groups) or postal zip codes. Finding target areas involves a population segment using selected demographics (e.g. households with income "greater than $80,000" and head of household an "average age of thirty-four to forty-five years"). Using the PCensus software, it will find and rank all the areas (places, census tracts, block groups, or zip codes) that have households that match this demographic profile or lifestyle (Census 2002).

The Department of Defense's **DARPA** (Defense Advanced Research Projects Agency) has a project called **LifeLog.** This project could be called a diary to end all diaries. It is a multimedia, digital record of places you go and things you see, hear, read, say, and touch. This item is being developed as one of the antiterrorism tools. However, DARPA does not consider LifeLog as an antiterrorism system but rather a tool to capture "one person's experience in and interactions with the world" through a camera, microphone, and sensors worn by the user. Everything from heartbeats to travel to Internet chatting would be recorded (LifeLog 2002).

LifeLog, now has existed for over a year, as one part of DARPA's research in **cognitive computing**. According to the information on the Web site, the research is fundamentally focused on developing revolutionary capabilities that would allow people to interact with computers in much more natural ways than those that exist today. The new generation of cognitive computers under development will understand their users and help them manage their affairs more effectively. The design of the research is to extend the model of a personal digital assistant (PDA) to one that might eventually become a personal digital partner (LifeLog 2003).

In an earlier discussion in this section, **William W. Agresti** pointed out how, today, our data silos are overflowing. The editor of *Computerworld* explained that globally, there was a 30 percent increase in stored information (of all sorts) from 1999 to 2002. Storage on hard disk drives rose 114 percent. He said, "Storage is the fastest growing capital cost within the data center in many enterprises." He also concluded that data centers will double their storage needs every eighteen to twenty-three months. Government agencies such as the IRS have been concerned about records storage since the beginning of the computer age (Betts 2003).

According to Robert L. Scheier, new rules are forcing companies to **buy more storage** and develop new policies around its use. Because of corporate scandals and privacy concerns, new laws and regulations require organizations to store more data, keep it longer, and make sure that it is accurate and easy to retrieve. The **Health Insurance Portability and Accountability Act (HIPAA),** enacted in August 1996, had a compliance deadline of April 2006. The industries affected are health care insurers, health claims clearinghouses, and health care providers. HIPAA encourages the use of electronic transactions to increase efficiencies in the health care field. It requires that medical records be kept in their original form for two years after the patient's death. Patient information is to be protected and made available in case of disasters. The other new regulatory enactment is the **Sarbanes-Oxley Act**, also called **Sarbox**, enacted August 2002 with a compliance deadline of April 2005. It primarily affects accounting firms that audit the financial statements of publicly traded companies, although the companies themselves may wish to retain the records (Scheier 2003).

Christopher Koch feels that the Sarbanes-Oxley compliance efforts are eating up CIO (chief information officer) time and budgets. Worse, in his opinion, CIOs are being regulated to a purely tactical role, which may be the CFOs (chief financial officers) plan. If this becomes true, CFOs would have control over one of the largest fixed costs in the company: information technology (Koch 2004).

Regulatory compliance issues and business needs are challenging IT (information technology) managers to change their storage strategies and move toward **information life-cycle management (ILM),** an automated policy that manages data from the cradle to the grave. ILM's goal: is to put certain types of data on appropriate types of storage devices and media depending on how long the data must be kept or how soon the data will need to be retrieved. Granted, ILM is still in its infancy; however, present methods of storage must be improved to meet the new regulatory compliance requirements (Mearian 2003b).

In addition to the mandated storage center, a backup data center has become a necessity. Conflicting recommendations have appeared as to how far the backup center should be located from the main data center. The distance seems to involve the geographical area and the value of the backup data. The most important concept is that the data are backed up and stored at an alternate site (Hamblen 2003).

Now that many of the problems of data management have been enumerated, it is obvious that organizations need to recognize that **data storage** should be managed like a resource, with a strategy in place and a dedicated staff. One approach is to invest in data storage management tools for capacity and determine who is consuming the data and who accessed it last. Another approach is data segmentation into two or three discrete tiers based on usage, archival requirements, and storage media. The dedicated staff is most important for technical advice and guidance in the application of sound data storage management. The requirements are organization-wide in an area that, in most instances, has not had sufficient managerial attention (Datz 2003).

Most IT executives would prefer **magnetic tape storage** to go away. Managing tape backup systems with slow and unreliable restoration, cartridge inventorying, and off-site storage problems have made executives hope for cheap disk drives to replace the fifty-year-old tape technology. Most of them think that they only need tape for cases where data can not be restored from disk. Most believe it is a necessary evil. In spite of the advances of disk arrays for backing up business data, there is no end in sight to the use of tape in the data center, especially for archival storage (Mearian 2003a).

Natural Language Processing (NLP)—according to *Webster's New World Computer Dictionary tenth edition* is—"in artificial intelligence, the use of a computer to decipher or analyze human language" (Webster 2003b). The objective of the Microsoft Natural Language Processing group is to build software that will analyze, understand, and generate languages that humans use naturally, so that eventually you will be able to address your computer as though you were addressing another person (NLP 2004). Several decades ago, in the 1970s and 1980s, pioneering examples of what, perhaps, today is called NLP were called fourth-generation languages or 4GLs. James Martin was the leading proponent of the 4GL era (Martin 1985).

The objective of the **Microsoft Natural Language Processing** group is not easy to reach because "understanding" language means, among other things, knowing what concepts a word or phrase stands for and knowing how to link

17

those concepts together in a meaningful way. Natural language is easiest for humans to learn and use; however, it is hardest for a computer to master. The group in addressing the problems uses a mix of knowledge-engineered and statistical and machine-learning techniques to disambiguate and respond to natural language input. Their work has implications for applications like text critiquing, information retrieval, question answering, summarization, gaming, and translation. Progress is being made; however, it is much slower than most like to tolerate (NLP 2004).

End User Development (EUD) is a similar concept to Natural Language Processing except that it is about taking control—not only of personalizing computer applications (end user computing) and writing programs—but designing new computer-based applications without ever seeing the underlying program code. EUD can also be described as do-it-yourself computing with the goal to empower users to design and create without the need for trained programmers or IT departments. Of course, the downside is **outsourcing** development efforts to end users, who must agonize over learning to program. The September, 2004 issue of *Communications of the ACM* has a special section of ten articles bringing together for the readers an in-depth look into the social and business issues of EUD as well as presenting cutting-edge technology to make EUD easier and more effective for all (Sutcliffe and Mehandjiev 2004).

In recent decades, **EUD has migrated** to customizable and extendable applications. Enterprise resource planning (ERP) and component-based solutions require teams of experts to build new applications. While technology has delivered the potential for end user control, it is still too difficult to use. Several technical, managerial, and social challenges must be solved to make EUD tools easier to use. Controlling and promoting EUD has been a management challenge for years. The critical issues involve motivating end users to adopt the technology, controlling development to minimize risks, creating maintainable software, and eliminating inaccurate and contradictory information. Tension between quality assurance and design freedom will always color advances in EUD, but new approaches are emerging. There must be improvement in technology if EUD is to escape its current niche of highly motivated users willing to endure the pain barrier associated with learning to program. End users in the scientific area currently do this with standard languages like C++ and Java, but business users generally do not venture beyond tailoring spreadsheets. Therefore, the quest is for easier programming languages (Sutcliffe and Mehandjiev 2004).

The BASIC programming language and the first personal computers were where EUD began and then progressed through information centers and fourth-generation languages just as NLP, described above. There were over one hundred 4GL languages developed, but most fell by the wayside. Among the most common **4GLs** were FOCUS, INTELLECT, LINC, MANTIS, NOMAD, and RAMIS. The 4GLs were used initially to access databases with English-like queries—"find all records where the name is Miller." The 4GLs were capable of taking the inquiry of the end user and automatically developing the necessary query program in, for example, COBOL, or other language. This capability probably caused part of the downfall of 4GLs because of fear of job loss by COBOL programmers and those instructors who taught COBOL. The 4GL program might require ten lines of code while the COBOL program would probably require over a hundred lines. In addition to simple-query 4GLs, some were used for report generation, for use with graphics, others used decision-support capabilities, and a few supported the analysis of data up to nine dimensions.

FOCUS is one of the early 4GLs developed by Information Builders Inc. Since January 1991, FOCUS report writer has been in use at Youngstown State University as a dependable and stable tool with over five thousand FOCUS jobs in circulation. At YSU, FOCUS is used for everything from ad hoc reporting to state data reporting. The university has over thirty FOCUS jobs running on a daily basis in production, helping to support materials management, general accounting, and institutional research to name a few departments (FOCUS 2004).

By the mid-1990s, **Martin Goetz** suggested that the reason everyone was not choosing 4GLs for enterprise development was that 4GLs did not come from the dominant software and hardware companies. Because many run interpretively and are inefficient at execution time, 4GLs have had their problems. Some may be tied to a particular database management system or operating system. Publicity may be another factor as consulting firms may hesitate to recommend 4GLs for in-house development because their skills are not needed (Goetz 1996).

A fifth generation of computer systems during the period of 1984 to 1990 has been characterized mainly by the acceptance of parallel processing. This generation saw the introduction of machines with hundreds of processors that could all be working on different parts of a single program. Semiconductor chips with a million components became available, and the use of semiconductor memories became standard on all computers (5GL Fifth Generation 1984-1990).

Transitions between generations in computer technology are hard to define. The year 1990 has been selected as a cutoff as many of the developments in computer systems since that time reflect gradual improvements over established systems making it hard to claim they represent a transition to a new "generation." However, a **sixth generation (1990-)** has been identified primarily due to the explosive growth of wide-area networking. Bandwidth continues to expand with T3 or larger transmission rates recognized as standard for regional networks and OC-3 or larger used as "backbone" for national interconnection for the regional networks. Two significant pieces of legislation: the High Performance Computing Act of 1991 and Senator Gore's Information Infrastructure and Technology Act of 1992 were significant (Sixth Generation 1990-).

Data warehousing is a collection of related databases that have been stored together so that the maximum value can be extracted from them. The basic idea of data warehousing is gathering as much related data as possible in the expectation that a meaningful picture will emerge through the use of **data mining**. Rather than using traditional database queries, which form search questions using a query language like SQL, data mining proceeds by classifying and clustering data from a variety of different and even mutually incompatible databases and then looking for associations. However, the use of data warehousing provides an environment where the data are related. In this environment, data-mining techniques enable programmers to collate and extract meaningful data from the warehouse by means of a technique called "drilldown." The data-mining software allows data warehouse users to see as much detail or summarization as they need to support their decision making through the use of decision support systems (DSS). These are complex programs designed to help corporate management discover the information needed to make decisions (Data Warehousing/Mining 2003).

Data mining is gaining recognition, not yet as a separate discipline, but in education, there are many meetings, and a number of software packages available. Online education in data mining is available at both Massachusetts Institute of Technology and Stanford University. Data mining education in United States and Canada is available in about a dozen universities including George Mason University, University of Central Florida, and the University of Toronto. In Europe, courses are offered at Ghent University in Belgium, University of Bristol in the United Kingdom, University of Granada in Spain, and the University of Lyon in France (Education 2004).

Kansas State University has a **laboratory for knowledge discovery in databases (KDD)** organized as a research group in the Computing and Information Sciences (CIS) Department. The research is in the areas of applied artificial intelligence (AI) and knowledge-based software engineering (KBSE) for decision support systems, machine learning, data mining, and knowledge discovery from large, spatial, and temporal databases (Hsu 2003).

Meetings and conferences in data mining and knowledge discovery are well organized and publicized. For example: a premiere conference on knowledge discovery and data mining in Seattle, August 22-25, 2004, three colocated major AI conferences in Banff, Canada, other meetings and conferences in Leipzig, Germany; Perugia, Italy; San Jose, United States of America; and Sheffield, United Kingdom (Meetings 2004).

Among the many data-mining and knowledge-discovery **software packages** available, **Clementine,** a data mining workbench enables the user to quickly develop predictive models using business expertise and deploy them into business operations to improve decision making. Clementine is designed around the de facto industry standard for data mining—CRISP-DM (Clementine 2004).

CiteSeer, a scientific literature digital library, is designed to improve the dissemination and feedback of scientific literature and to provide improvements in functionality, usability, availability, cost, comprehensiveness, efficiency, and timeliness. Instead of creating just another digital library, CiteSeer provides algorithms, techniques, and software that can be used in other digital libraries. It also indexes PostScript and PDF research articles on the Web. CiteSeer uses autonomous citation indexing (ACI) to create a citation index that can be used for literature search and evaluation. The way that researchers access scientific information on the World Wide Web is being revolutionized. Articles are being made available on the homepages of authors or institutions at journal Web sites or in online archives. Because scientific information on the Web is largely disorganized, the creation of digital libraries incorporating the use of ACI creates useful citation indices (CiteSeer 2003).

The cover story for the January 2004 *IEEE Spectrum* entitled **"A Fountain of Knowledge 2004 Will Be the Year of the Analysis Engine,"** describes that the great strength of computers is that they can reliably manipulate vast amounts of data very quickly; unfortunately, computers cannot discern what any of that data actually means. IBM Corporation is about to make a major breakthrough in the field of machine understanding, called **Web Fountain**, an analysis engine. At present, search engines are the standard tools for dealing with the increasing glut of information. Google is the present leading search engine. Search engines direct the user to a small selection of documents that simply contain words that match a set of search terms. Instead of another search engine, what is needed is an **analysis engine** that can discern a document's meaning and then provide insight into what the search results mean in aggregate. This is what IBM is about to deliver. The major advantage of Web Fountain will be its ability to automatically structure the data to be used (Cass 2004).

Text retrieval conferences (TREC) were started in 1992, cosponsored by the National Institute of Standards and Technology (NIST) and the U.S. Department of Defense. The main purpose was to support research within the information retrieval community by providing the infrastructure necessary for large-scale evaluation of text retrieval methodologies. The following goals are important to the TREC workshop series: to encourage research in information retrieval; to increase communications among industry, academia, and government; to speed the transfer of technology from research labs into commercial products; and to increase the availability of appropriate evaluation techniques. A program committee of representatives from government, industry, and academia oversee TREC. The TREC yearly cycle ends with a workshop that is a forum for participants to share their experiences. This evaluation effort has grown from year to year and by 2003 had ninety-three groups representing twenty-two countries. TREC's dual goals of improving the state-of-the-art information retrieval and facilitating technology transfer are being met (TREC 2004).

For someone who lived through the use of punched-card data entry, it was impossible for me to omit an example of technology advancement. The example is the full-size **projection keyboard** for handheld devices. It is a keyboard made entirely of light projected onto desktops; airplane tray tables; even kitchen counters with functions, feels, and sounds like its mechanical counterpart. In spite of the advances in the technologic interacting with today's computers, cell phones, and personal digital assistants, the miniature displays and keyboards are too small for human hands and eyesight. In 1999, a member of the Canesta Inc. team, who is also on the computer science faculty at Duke University, proposed using a single tiny sensor to observe the user's fingers, transforming motion into keystrokes. The projection keyboard, developed during the past four years, will soon be available in cell phones and PDAs and may also replace laptop mechanical keyboards. The manufacturer has reduced the system to three components—a projector, an infrared light source, and a sensing system. Each component is about the size of a pencil eraser. Together, the cost to the user will be less than the folding mechanical keyboard and will draw less power than a cell phone. The projection system feels almost like a mechanical keyboard, even if users feel only the impact of their fingers on the projection surface when typing (Tomasi 2003).

INFORMATION

INFORMATION IS DEFINED in *Webster's New World Computer Dictionary* tenth edition 2003 as "information data whether in the form of numbers, graphics, or words that has been organized, systematized, and presented so that the underlying patterns become clear. The temperature, humidity, and wind reports from hundreds of weather stations are data; a computer simulation that shows how these data predict a strong possibility of tornadoes is information" (Webster 2003b).

From the previous discussion of data, we were convinced, or should have been convinced, that due to the growing volume of data, there is much to be done to convert it into **usable information**. We need to recognize that specific data are not usable and should no longer be maintained, but individuals are reluctant to take responsibility for the destruction or identity of data that are no longer needed. This is where our previous discussion of storage becomes relevant; data storage needs to be managed like a resource with a strategy in place and a dedicated staff.

Note that a number of the following subjects do not relate directly to information; however, they are included to provide the reader with current descriptions of many subjects involved in providing information from data.

SPAM is the well-known name for all the unsolicited and unwanted advertising e-mail that makes use of the Internet throughout the world. After the public complaining about SPAM for a number of years, Congress passed and the president signed legislation effective Jnuary 1, 2004. The act may be cited as the "Controlling the Assault of Nonsolicited Pornography and Marketing Act of 2003" or the CAN-SPAM Act of 2003 (SPAM Laws 2003).

Since the **SPAM legislation**, all reports indicate that e-mail usage is declining because users are dissatisfied with the lack of any noticeable reduction in SPAM. They seem to be convinced that the legislation will not reduce SPAM and may be counterproductive because it overrides other states' proposed legislation that had tougher approaches to dealing with SPAM (Article Central 2004).

Blogs are amateur Web sites that are fast, funny, and totally biased. In 1997 the word "blog" was coined to work as either a noun or verb, short for Web log, and used to describe a Web site where one could post daily scribbling, journal style, about any topic mostly critiquing and linking together articles online that may have sparked interest. By 2002, Pyra Labs, the maker of software for operating blogs, claimed 970,000 users. The first major accomplishment by bloggers was keeping the Trent Lot story alive about his comments at Strom Thurmond's one hundredth birthday party after the big newspapers and TV networks had dropped it. Lot was out as Senate majority leader, and blogs had drawn their first blood (Grossman 2004).

A blogger needs only an Internet access and a computer, and it helps to have a personal obsession and total confidence in your own voice. Less than ten years ago, practically all media was still a one-way street, then self-publishing online journals, or Web logs, began to let bloggers bypass the corporate media gatekeepers to say and show practically anything they could think of to tens of millions of computer users around the world. Bloggers had only themselves to please, and they began enthusiastically linking and cross-linking to and referencing one another's sites and commentaries. These links drove development of blog technology, as well as user curiosity and ultimately creation of the worldwide blogosphere. Technorati Inc., a Web log-tracking company, reports of almost 4.2 million Web logs worldwide as of October 2004, up from about one million a year earlier. The availability of commercial software, easy to use for developing blogs, has made the term synonymous with "personal Web site" (Rosenbloom 2004).

Among all U.S. libraries, **Library of Congress** is the leader. It is too large and too complex for a detailed discussion in this section; however, if you, the reader, are not familiar with the resources available, you should go to its home page *http://www.loc.gov/* and see for yourself. The digital collections programs are impressive. Even though this is only one functional area, it is impossible not to point it out. For example, American memory, a single digital area, now offers more than 7.5 million digital items from more than one hundred historical collections.

Libraries have long been recognized as the information centers of schools, cities, corporations, and private businesses. An example of improvements that have taken place in a school library is the Ablah Library at Wichita State University. It is now the **Wichita State University Libraries Information System**, made up of a total of seven libraries, including the Ablah Library. The system is one of 120 members of the American Research Libraries (ARL), a not-for-profit membership organization comprised of the leading research libraries in North America. The ARL mission is to shape and influence forces affecting the future of research libraries in the process of scholarly communication. Their programs and services promote equitable access to the effective use of recorded knowledge in support of teaching, research, scholarship, and community service. Brian Hawkins would be proud to see how well the Wichita State University Libraries Information System has carried out many or most of his ideas that he included in his national electronic model recommended in 1994.

The **Wichita State University Libraries Information System** has over one hundred databases available and all searchable by title and subject. The software used to access these databases includes: First Search, Info Track, SilverPlatter, LexisNexis both academic and statistical, and Wilson Web. The majority of the library information is now available electronically. In addition to the electronic databases are course reserves, e-journals, e-books, e-news sources, virtual reference shelf, digital collections, and other e-resources by subject. The library catalog is supported by a software package called Voyager from the vendor Endeavor Information Systems. The WSU library system has remained on the same organizational level as other academic departments with a dean of libraries, associate deans, and typical departmental organization. The university has a CIO who supervises the university computing, telecommunications functions and media resources (WSU 2003).

In my original 1994 report, I recommended that the K-12 schools become the **centers of their communities** with **year-round operation**. Since academic libraries have always been the information centers for academic institutions, it seems natural for cities with branch libraries to consolidate them in available schools with year-round access for both students, parents, and the public. When the branch libraries are located within schools operated year-round, the cities must be held accountable for the supervision of library visitors to prevent undesirable individuals from entering the schools.

Until recently, nearly anyone could come to a college library and gain **free access to a computer** and cruise the Internet with little chance of being identified. Now a number of college libraries require students to log in to use the computer, and visitors are authenticated by a name and password in order to use the computer. When authentication systems are required, law enforcement and government authorities can more easily trace network activity to a particular person (Carlson 2004a).

The education industry must not fail to recognize that **students are its most valuable resource.** Unfortunately, many students entering college do not meet a common level of accepted standards. As a result, colleges must provide remedial courses for what the students failed to learn in high school. Another problem concerns gifted students, the leaders in their classes who have unusual talents. The National Assessment of Educational Progress has observed that by setting a minimum standard, and holding all students accountable for reaching that low level, a ceiling has been placed on both expectations and outcomes.

The National Association for Gifted Children has promoted gifted programs; however, funds are needed from the Javits Grants (Spielhagen 2005).

The level of creativity is much higher among students than many administrators and faculties appreciate. Unfortunately, many of our creative students are never recognized and are dismissed as eccentrics or troublemakers. The existing programs seem to recognize those good students that have previously been recognized from one grade to another. Many not so recognized are creative students and need assistance for their future development. Many of these unrecognized students have a high degree of creativity and make good prospects to appreciate the **visualization of data** to provide information.

In the present situation of information overload, **visualization software** is useful in cutting through the clutter. This software can take vast amounts of data and organize it in interactive graphical format pictures that make the information much easier to grasp and explore thoroughly. Executives around the world in a broad range of industries are finding that information-visualization software helps them make critical business decisions by cutting through information overload. One example of visualization software used in the public sector is at the U.S. agriculture department's National Agricultural Statistics Service (NASS) in Fairfax, Virginia. The NASS Web site provides information on agricultural trends in hundreds of statistical tables and charts. Through the use of Insight Software Inc. of Sunnyvale, California, the information is made much more coherent and meaningful (Borzo 2004).

Edward R. Tufte has written seven books including the leading books on visualization of data to provide information. He has his own self-publishing company that has received many awards for their content and design. He is professor emeritus at Yale University where he taught courses in statistical evidence, information design, and interface design. His current work includes digital videos, sculpture, and printmaking. In my opinion, he made famous the classic work of **Charles Joseph Minard** (1781-1870), the French engineer, who, in a chart, shows the terrible fate of Napoleon's army in Russia. Minard's work has been described as seeming to defy the pen of the historian by its brutal eloquence. This combination of data map and time series, drawn in 1861, and shown in figure 1, portrays the devastating losses suffered in Napoleon's Russian campaign of 1812. Beginning at the Polish-Russian border near the Niemen River, he used a thick black band that shows the size of the army 422,000 men as it invaded Russia in June 1812. The size of the army is shown at each place on the map by the width of the band. By September, the army reached Moscow with only one hundred thousand men. Moscow, at the time, was sacked and deserted. The band narrowed to show the losses. A darker and lower band was used to show the path of Napoleon's retreat from Moscow, which linked to a temperature scale and dates at the bottom of the chart. Many men froze on the march out of Russia because it was a bitterly cold winter. The graphic shows the crossing of the Berezina River by the struggling army into Poland with only ten thousand men remaining. The movements of auxiliary troops are shown as they sought to protect the rear and the flank of the advancing army. The graphic tells a rich, coherent story with its multivariate data, far more enlightening than just a single number bounding along over time. Minard plotted six variables, the size of the army, its location on a two-dimensional surface, direction of the army's movement, and temperature on various dates during the retreat from Moscow. Tufte points out that this statistical graphic may be the best ever drawn (Tufte 2001).

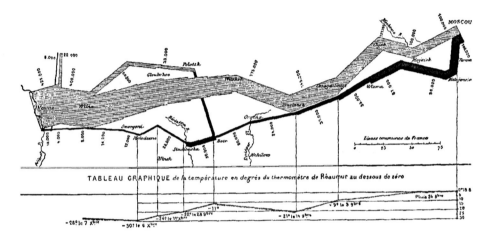

Figure 1
Napoleon's Russian campaign 1812-1813
Source: Edward R. Tufte, *The Visual Display of Quantitative Information,*
Graphics Press, Second Edition, 2001.

Dedicated staffs to manage information have been in existence for a number of years. A pioneer in this area was the **information resource manager** or **IRM**. This position originated with the enactment of the Paperwork Reduction Act of 1980. The act established the Office of Information and Regulatory Affairs in the Office of Management and Budget. The law also provided that each federal agency designate a senior official reporting directly to each agency head, to carry out the information management responsibilities of the agency. This individual became known as the information resource manager or IRM. Many corporate and other organizations followed with IRM appointments and dedicated staffs.

The enactment of the National Defense Authorization Act for Fiscal Year 1996, known as the **Cohen Act**, also as the Clinger-Cohen Act, practically eliminated the appointment of information resource managers. This came about due to the provisions of the Cohen Act that assigned the responsibility for the use of information technology for federal programs to the director of management and budget. This official is also responsible for the implementation of the executive order that established the **CIO (chief information officer) council** composed of CIOs and deputy CIOs of executive agencies. **The Cohen Act established the position of CIO** in twenty-three federal departments and agencies. The end result was the elimination of the position of IRM and the substitution of CIO. The *CIO Magazine,* along with the Cohen Act, in combination, brought about the change from **IRM to CIO.** I pioneered teaching a graduate course in information resources management in 1980 prior to the president's signature on the act itself. In retrospect, the leadership in the CIO area supported by the Cohen Act brought many advantages never attained by the IRM leadership. This has been good for the country as a whole.

The **Chief Information Officers Council** has demonstrated its leadership in a number of ways. One example was a report requested by a panel of the National Academy of Public Administration. The report was entitled "The Transforming Power of Information Technology: Making the Federal Government an Employer of Choice for IT Employees." The recommendation contained in the report was: "that the federal government transition to a market-based human resources management system for IT (information technology) professionals that would, in general, make the federal government an employee of choice for IT employees" (NAPA 2001).

With the encouragement and leadership of the **Chief Information Officers Council,** there are two schools currently in operation that are educating CIOs for the future. One school is the Information Resources Management College, a holdover from the former IRM concept before the Cohen Act's CIO directive. The establishment of the certificate program has seen the National Defense University graduate three hundred federal employees and expects that nearly 30 percent of the CIO program students will come from civilian agencies next year. The IRM College focuses on midlevel systems managers because it is thought that they are the future of federal leadership. Through agreements with Carnegie Mellon University, George Mason University, George Washington University, and the University of Maryland's University College, the CIO University has as many as two thousand students. The IRM College began making CIO program courses available on the Web. For the online courses, the college uses Blackboard 5, an educational portal package, used by many colleges and universities (Murray 2003).

Another example of the council's leadership was the establishment of **SmartBUY** in June 2003, the federal, government-wide software-enterprise licensing program initiated by the Office of Management and Budget and executed by General Services Administration. Although it was directed that all federal agencies use the program, it will take time to enact SmartBUY agreements. The program does not require a software purchase "freeze." It does provide for migration to SmartBUY agreements but will not be accomplished by forced breaking of existing agreements. Agencies should not shut down normal operations since SmartBUY will not have wide coverage of software titles for sometime. SmartBUY agreements do not apply to all software, only to commercially available, commodity-type, and listed on a Web site and made available only to authorized agencies (SmartBUY 2003).

The navy department chief information officer was chosen as a representative of the twenty-three departments and agencies included in the Cohen Act. The vision, mission, and goals are all included on the Web site with a reference to the strategic plan FY 2004-2005 (CIO Navy 2003).

The **state of Utah chief information officer** was selected to represent a state CIO who is responsible for vision, strategy, direction, guidelines, policies, planning, coordination, and oversight for information technology for the executive branch of the state government. The CIO reports to the governor and is a member of the governor's senior staff, cabinet council, and works with department and IT executives across the state (CIO Utah 2003).

In my 1999 update report, I described the New York based **research board** as the most prestigious research organization in the field of information management. Apparently, it still is. The board is one of the best kept secrets in that the Web site is a single page that points out that membership is by invitation only and restricted to chief information officers of the world's largest corporations. Since my 1999 report, I have only been able to find one article about the research board. It described a rare interview by Maryfran Johnson, editor in chief of *Computerworld* when she interviewed Peter Sole, CEO of the research board. In the interview she disclosed that many of the members are not IT specialists in that they are businesspeople with IT as a part of their portfolio. They are concerned with not only IT, but with other responsibilities like logistics, operations, supply chain, e-business initiatives, even venture capital funds set up to develop relationships with leading-edge companies. According to Sole, all members sit on the executive committee of the board and, without exception, they are seen as one of the senior management team. Their key responsibility is making sure their companies get maximum benefit from IT investments (Johnson 2001).

Chief information officer (CIO) is one of the many "chiefs" organizations use in their makeup. *CIO Magazine* conducted a third annual "state of the CIO" survey in 2004 and obtained over five hundred responses disclosing that for CIOs right now it is the best of times and the worst of times. These two extremes create a sense of unease in many CIOs about their responsibilities, their stature, and their future. The number who report to their CFO is on the rise; however, what really matters is whether or not the CIO is a member of the executive team and a valued company player (Lundberg 2004).

CFO, "chief financial officer," is a commonly used term with the position well identified and accepted by nearly everyone. This cannot be said about a number of other chiefs. Three years ago over a dozen were identified (Rosenthal 2001).

CAO	Administration	CMO	Marketing or Maintenance
CBO	Budget	COO	Operating
CCO	Creative	CPO	Privacy
CFO	Financial	CRO	Risk
CGO	Growth	CSO	Strategy
CKO	Knowledge	CTO	Technology

I have not been able to determine the number of organizations actually using the position of chief knowledge officer. Over a decade ago it was hard to find the number using the position "chief information officer." Through the years, the number of CIOs has increased as many individuals are actually filling the CIO positions.

We will look at one example to gain an understanding of how these various titles really work. A few years ago the term "chief privacy officer" (CPO) was unknown. Corporate counsel handled privacy-related matters. With one organization, a number of privacy-related problems damaged the public perception and stock price of some companies. The company accidentally exposed the names and telephone numbers of some customers to other Internet users causing a problem with United Parcel Services' new Web-based product return system. This is a typical example of problems directed toward the CPO (Kelly 2001).

The CPO issue has not been a sudden idea that gradually goes away after a few years, as shown by the appointment of Ms. Nuala O'Connor Kelly as chief privacy officer of the Department of Homeland Security by Secretary Ridge on April 18, 2003. She is responsible, among numerous other duties, for privacy compliance across the organization, including assuring that the technologies sustain and do not erode privacy protections relating to the use, collection, and disclosure of personal information (DHS Organization 2003).

The chief learning officer (CLO) was not included in the above Rosenthal list. The first record of a chief learning officer was an article dated May 1996 (Willets 1996). During the years since the early appointments of CLOs, along with many other "chiefs," I did not give this area much attention. During the interim, I have found that the idea has quite a following being led by the development and publication of the *Chief Learning Officer* magazine. The magazine organized and held the 2004 chief learning officer symposium

"Managing the Business of Enterprise Learning." There is also a chief learning officer's series of e-seminars to provide interaction with industry experts on the tools, technologies, issues, and ideas that fuel enterprise education. The magazine also provides a SourceBook as a free search engine listing hundreds of leading companies providing products, services, tools, and expertise. White papers provide in-depth information on what today's leading organizations are doing to promote workforce learning and development (CLO 2003).

David Skyrme, after reviewing a number of definitions of **"learning organizations,"** developed the following definition: "Learning organizations are those that have in place systems, mechanisms and processes, that are used to continually enhance their capabilities and those who work with it or for it, to achieve sustainable objectives—for themselves and the communities in which they participate." However, the definition is followed by the answer to the question "Why the Interest in 'Learning Organizations'?" as "Basically, it's the search for the [unattainable] Holy Grail. Companies are seeking to improve existing products and services [continuous improvement], and innovation [breakthrough strategies]. This has resulted in a plethora of initiatives such as TQM [total quality management] and BPR [business process reengineering]" (Skyrme, n.d.).

One of the major problems most CIOs encounter is **outsourcing**, the transfer of work or services to an external contractor often in a foreign land. Outsourcing is a typical problem in Wichita, Kansas, due to the constant problem of whether or not airplane parts are to be manufactured locally by the company requiring the parts, by a local subcontractor, or by a contractor in some foreign land (Tarpy 2003). CIOs, like most other managers, are constantly under pressure to reduce costs and cut budgets including personnel. The rapid advances in information technology add to the problems. Because computer-supported systems are involved in all manufacturing processes, and the CIO, in addition to all other duties, is the official most often approached for answers not only about information technology but the outsourcing, this becomes a major concern.

An example of some problems that can occur in a large company can be found at **Textron** which has forty-one business units, nine CIOs, all trying to operate under one standard. Textron is a $10.7 billion global enterprise that spends approximately $320 million on an information-technology services organization that it established in 2002. The IT community has gone through waves of decentralization followed by centralization. Right now the buzzword is **consolidation** (Overby 2003).

Initially, a decade ago, companies opted for a sole source approach to outsourcing for many large **information-technology outsourcing (ITO)** transactions requiring either complicated or rare sets of capabilities. Buyers were faced with limited selection because service providers with the desired capabilities and geographic presence were scarce. **Business process outsourcing (BPO)** has become a more accepted alternative. A recent poll indicated that 50 percent of organizations are more likely to consider a sole source approach to BPO than ITO. Conversely, 33 percent are less likely to select sole source approaches for BPO. Only 17 percent of the respondents indicated that the difference between BPO and ITO had little impact on their outsourcing approach. *The Outsourcing Journal* provides a wealth of information about outsourcing (Bender-Samuel 2003).

IBM recognizes that outsourcing has helped organizations trim costs and is willing to provide **business transformation outsourcing** services to help make outsourcing a strategic element in business transformation (IBM 2003). IBM is shopping for consulting business in its attempt to help business transformation; however, it directly supports BPO, referenced above (Bulkeley 2004b). In January 2004, IBM started using another term "**offshoring**" to describe the company's intended shift of three thousand jobs from various U.S. locations to China, India, and Brazil. IBM also announced that it expects to add fifteen thousand jobs worldwide during 2004, with a net total of five thousand of them in the United States (Bulkeley 2004a).

In outsourcing, **human factors** are one of the most important issues, particularly when the outsourcer is located offshore. Highly specialized skills can often be supplied by the outsourcer on a part-time basis. This often offsets the requirement to fill precious openings with staffers whose technical skills are required only intermittently. Any staffers, terminated and then hired by the outsourcer, find new opportunities to broaden their experiences across multiple industries. There are other benefits, such as the transfer of some administrative costs involved in "managing out" nonperforming staffers. On the other hand, outsourcing can cause fear and dysfunctional behavior in other remaining staff. When staffers see IT being outsourced, they may worry that they will be next. Before, be sure that there is a comprehensive plan in place to deal with the human factor (Perkins 2003).

Another interesting situation found in outsourcing was described in an article in the *Knowledge Management News* explaining the **phantom-limb sensation** that takes place in 80 percent of amputees; when a limb is lost, the individual continues to feel its presence long afterward. The authors explain how the brain remaps neural signals and inputs from other areas of the body to adapt to the loss of sensory information crossing of wires, as it were, to compensate. The article also describes how similar effects take place when outsourcing and key functions are cut off from information, knowledge, and skills of former employees. In the United Kingdom, the authors found that outsourcing is currently one of the biggest business trends (and highest growth sectors); in 2002 business-process outsourcing grew 28 percent (Willcocks 2003).

The **BPO** is growing in demand, and computer services firms are jockeying to grab larger and larger shares of the opportunity. In the past, BPO involved mostly back-office functions: running data centers, installing desktop PCs, and running applications. Now BPO is taking over payroll, travel services, customer service, and accounting. For example, IBM signed a ten-year $400-million contract to handle Procter and Gamble's human resources tasks. Another example is Accenture's five-year, $500-million contract to take over AT&T Corporation's credit and accounts-receivable management functions (Loftus 2003).

By the middle of 2004, **offshore outsourcing** was still gathering momentum according to a study completed by *CIO Magazine* with inputs from the Gartner Group. Out of 101 IT executives surveyed, 86 percent said they already had offshore application development, and 26 percent offshore their call centers. India's market share and that of other countries keeps growing; however, neighbors in Canada and Mexico are handling highly complex projects. New members of the European Union such as the Czech Republic, Poland, and Hungary are an enticing near shore option for Western European companies and Europe-based U.S. businesses (Datz 2004).

U.S. clients transfer knowledge to offshore vendors and include everything from hard skills to an understanding of what the company and its users expect from a system. This **knowledge transferred** can make or break an outsourced project. CIOs involved in outsourcing must understand the difference between the knowledge that must be transferred and the knowledge that must not be transferred. If this transfer of knowledge is not understood in the beginning of the offshore negotiations, there is much likelihood that problems will appear immediately. For example, can the client tell in advance the extent of the programming capabilities of the offshore vendor (Overby 2004)?

Another outsourcing resource is the **Outsourcing Institute**, a global professional association dedicated to outsourcing and providing a neutral source for unparalleled information, networking, resources, services, and solutions to help organizations achieve success in outsourcing (Institute 2003).

In a previous discussion, it was explained how the federal government had implemented the new method of software procurement using the SmartBUY e-commerce platform to permit government agencies and many others to browse, search, and purchase **software and services online** from approved government suppliers. In the nongovernment area a major change is taking place in the software industry. In 1999, Thomas Siebel of Siebel Systems launched the first attempt to offer software as a service when it established and spun off a business called Sales.com. On October 2, 2003, Siebel announced a partnership with IBM to offer software over the Internet as a low-cost monthly service (Bank and Bulkeley 2003).

Salesforce.com is going beyond CRM (customer relationship management) with no longer a one-size-fits-all solution. It is taking modularity down to the customer level and hopes to bring its hosted solution beyond CRM. Since the needs of most enterprises are looking for more customization, Salesforce.com introduced "sforce," an online application-development utility to enable companies to build business applications within the hosted software delivery system. Sforce is available as a Web-based service for a monthly user fee; it will enable developers to build applications on the sforce architecture using products like Microsoft Visual Studio, Borland's JBuilder, BEA WebLogic Workshop, and Sun's Java. Sforce also provides core application services like authentication, data management, document management, and text search. As the first product to be offered under a new brand, sforce represents an important extension for the company. The cost of sforce is $50 per user, per month, plus $1 per megabyte, per month, with the first three users 10 MB are free for the first year (Myron 2003).

A young student, **Linus Torvalds**, at the University of Helsinki in Finland, created **Linux** as a hobby. Linus had an interest in Minix, a small UNIX system, when he decided to develop a system that exceeded the Minix standards. His work began in 1991 when he released version 0.02. He worked steadily until 1994 when version 1.0 of the Linux Kernel was released. Development has continued under the GNU (an acronym for the open source version of the of the Unix operating system) General Public License and its source code is freely available to everyone. However, this does not mean Linux and its assorted distributions are free as companies, and developers may charge money for it as long as the source code remains available. Linux may be used for a wide variety of purposes including networking, software development, and as an end-user platform. Linux is often considered as an excellent, low-cost alternate to other more expensive operating systems. Linux's functionality and availability have made it quite popular worldwide. A large number of software programmers have taken the Linux source code and adapted it to their individual needs. There are dozens of ongoing projects for porting Linux to various hardware configurations and purposes. Over 123,000 Linux users have registered with the Linux Counter which has an estimated 18 million Linux users (Linux 2003).

IBM seized **Linux** as a way to sell more hardware and services and to delay Microsoft in corporate accounts. It is claimed that just about any kind of software can be found in open-source form. There is a Web site called SourceForce.net, a meeting place for programmers that is said to list eighty-six thousand programs in progress (Kirkpatrick 2004a).

Another change in the software industry is the threat of **open source databases**. The term "open source" means that the source code is provided as it was explained above for the Linux operating system. When the **source**

code is not provided, as happens with most software packages, changes in the software applications must go back to the provider in order to be made. This is because the source code is proprietary, and not released with the software package when purchased or leased. The open source databases pose threats to other database software packages and, in particular, to Larry Ellison's Oracle database software. Oracle database software is, by far, the leader in the database software portion of the software industry. In addition, the open-source database software also threatens all of the commercial database providers. Microsoft's SQL Server, which is generally targeted at smaller businesses, may be most immediately affected, but the premium price Oracle traditionally has been able to command as the market leader may have the farthest to fall (Bank 2003; Kirkpatrick 2004a).

According to David Bank, "Old Software programs never die they just open source." Software companies adopt the **open source** approach as a method for marketing and as a means to cut costs. Computer Associates International Inc., BEA Systems Inc., and Sun Microsystems Inc. each announced plans to offer products under open source licenses. This method generally makes the programs available for free and allows users to modify the underlying programming instructions, called source code, to meet their own needs (Bank 2004).

An earlier reference was made to William W. Agresti in the data section. He is also recommending a new methodology that he describes as "**discovery informatics.**" He defines the term as the study and practice of employing the full spectrum of computing, analytical science and technology to the singular pursuit of discovering new information by identifying and validating patterns in data. The Johns Hopkins University is planning a center for discovery informatics believing discovery can be enhanced by exploring synergies and leveraging approaches and technologies associated with a variety of disciplines and domains (Agresti 2003).

Professor Agresti describes discovery informatics as a methodology that should be recognized and included in the ACM (Association for Computing Machinery) classification system. Discovery informatics as a new entry under computing methodologies that includes information storage and retrieval, document and text processing, artificial intelligence, pattern recognition, and database management. Although the article points out that computing science and technology are relatively new, our terminology would have fit in comfortably in the world of 1620 when Francis Bacon described a path to new knowledge that began by bringing together the relevant data "particulars relating to the subject under inquiry" into tables of discovery (Agresti 2003).

Professor Peter Denning advocates the idea that information technology is on the way to becoming a recognized profession. He pushes the idea year after year in his column "The Profession of IT" that began in 2001 in

Communications of the ACM. Professor Denning has done more than anyone to gain the establishment of an **IT profession** (Denning 2001). Numerous schools now offer a major in information technology. One example is the U.S. Naval Academy. The Australian Computer Society has called on its government to support its bid to become the accreditation agency for the IT profession, making membership mandatory for computer staffers ranging from Microsoft certified engineers to high-level project managers (Riley 2004).

"Making Them Pay," was a headline in a technology report in the *Wall Street Journal* of March 22, 2004, that explained how online businesses are finally learning how to make money charging for information. Some companies, such as the *Wall Street Journal* have been charging for its *Wall Street Journal Online* (WSJ.com) that I have used for some time. Others include: AmericanGreetings.com (greeting cards), Consumerinfo.com (personal credit reports), Ancestry.com (genealogy), ConsumerReports.org (consumer guide), Real.com (news, sports, and entertainment), Match.com (making available millions of personal ads just like a print publication), Everequest.com (games), and GamesSpy.com (games). Sales of online content continue to increase. The Online Publishers Association, a New York-based trade group, estimates that U.S. consumers spent about $1.6 billion on online content last year, up from $1.3 billion in 2002. An estimate in the United Kingdom, 58 percent of the members of Online Publishers charge for content, and about half of the remainder have said they plan to begin charging the next year (Totty 2004).

The Internet has spoiled us all into thinking that all information should be free. This article about making them pay opens the door for the future of many business opportunities. To take advantage of charging for information, it appears to boil down to a marketing problem. To be successful, the information for sale must be unobtainable else-where, or not in the time frame the customer desires. Sports information is an example. The digitization of the many books by several leading efforts may be used as an example of the information not being available else-where. These are only introductory steps (with no mention of pricing) necessary in the development of a successful marketing plan; however, they are sufficient to lead the way toward the many opportunities that are available.

KNOWLEDGEMANAGEMENT

KNOWLEDGE MANAGEMENT (KM) has often been referred to as a fad; however, the term has existed for a number of years. Before the term was recognized, there were numerous examples of knowledge workers as Professor Peter Drucker predicted when individuals, as **knowledge profiteers**, took advantage of the information they had, using it as knowledge to make fortunes. Early examples, years prior to Drucker, included Nathan Rothschild, Cyrus McCormick, and George Westinghouse. The one thing knowledge profiteers need to follow is that in order to turn a data stream into profitable knowledge, the profiteers need to remain focused on the right details. Warren Buffett is a leading example of this application. Another modern day example of a knowledge profiteer is Bill Gates (Fuld 1998).

The term "knowledge management" goes back much further than anything I found in the current knowledge management literature. My old friend Woody Horton, the author of the textbook I used when I taught the first graduate course in information resources management, documented the **origin of knowledge management.** He gives credit to Sir Stafford Beer for a report entitled "Managing Modern Complexity" and a committee on science and astronautics, U.S. House of Representatives, Ninety-first Congress, Second Session, January 27, 1970, 43-44. From the same source, I learned that Henry Nichols authored "Bureaucracy, Technology, and Knowledge Management." The article was published in the *Public Administration Review,* for a symposium on knowledge management, Nov.-Dec. 1975, pp. 572-576. And also, from Woody's book, that J. F. Berry and C. M. Cook are the authors of *Managing Knowledge as a Corporate Resource,* dated May 28, 1976. I was surprised but pleased to learn that the Public Administration Society sponsored a symposium on knowledge management in 1975 (Horton 1979).

In 1994, Stan Davis and Jim Botkin published **"The Coming of Knowledge-Based Business"** in the *Harvard Business Review.* In summary, the article indicated that economic growth was going to come from knowledge-based businesses that have learned to convert information into knowledge and use it to provide a competitive edge. The article also served as an introduction to their book *The Monster under the Bed*. The book's extended title is *How Business Is Mastering the Opportunity of Knowledge for Profit* (Davis and Botkin 1994).

The following discussion was taken from "**The ABC's of Knowledge Management**" at the CIO Knowledge Management Research Center:

"**What is Knowledge Management?** Unfortunately, there is no universal definition of KM, just as there's no agreement as to what constitutes knowledge in the first place. For this reason, it's best to think of KM in the broadest context. Succinctly put, KM is the process through which organizations generate value from their intellectual and knowledge-based assets. Most often, generating value from such assets involves sharing them among employees, departments and even with other companies in an effort to devise best practices. It's important to note that the definition says nothing about technology; while KM is often facilitated by IT, technology by itself is not KM." The article continues with a simplified example of a knowledge worker, a golf caddie, who does more than carry clubs and track down wayward balls. A good caddie will give advice to golfers, when asked. He may explain that the wind makes the ninth hole play fifteen yards longer. When the golfer takes advantage of the advice, he may well want to play the course again or increase the tip for the caddie. When good caddies are willing to share their tips and knowledge, the caddie master may use KM to make the system better for all caddies and for the reputation and use of the course as well (Santosus and Surmacz n.d.).

Another definition: "Knowledge Management is the explicit and systematic management of vital knowledge—and its associated processes of creation, organization, diffusion, use and exploitation"—a definition that includes some critical aspects of any successful knowledge management program (Skyrme n.d.).

Tacit knowledge is the hardest part of implementing knowledge management. The word "**tacit**," according to the dictionary, means something implied but not expressed, understood, or stated openly (*Encarta*). It is knowledge that we have in our heads. When the word "knowledge" is substituted for the word "something," tacit knowledge includes those thoughts or ideas that are carried in a person's brain but not recorded and many times not discussed.

Explicit knowledge, according to the dictionary means expressing all details in a clear and obvious way, leaving no doubt as to the intended meaning (*Encarta*). Explicit knowledge is typically recorded in books, libraries, newspapers, magazines, computer databases, Web sites, disks, CDs, and CD-RWs.

Moving tacit to explicit knowledge is a major problem in knowledge management because the management of tacit knowledge implies the management of people who have the tacit knowledge in their heads. Ideally, it is a matter of finding the tacit knowledge known by those individuals who possess it and convincing them to share their tacit knowledge so that it will become explicit knowledge and available to all (Nonaka and Takeuchi 1995).

Expert systems are known for moving tacit knowledge to explicit knowledge. Through the years, major efforts have been made to develop knowledge-based systems in the field of artificial intelligence (AI). These knowledge-based systems are one branch of artificial intelligence known as expert systems. An expert system uses the expertise of human experts, called **knowledge engineers**, who are knowledgeable in the specific area and able to obtain the knowledge used by the expert to build the knowledge base used by the expert system. Diplomacy and the use of cognitive psychology are more important to the knowledge engineer in obtaining the knowledge from the expert than other technical skills. An inference mechanism as a part of the expert system makes inferences based on its interpretation of the representation of the expert's knowledge. Rules were the most common form of knowledge representation in the early expert systems. In some respects, rules were used that were similar to if-then statements of programming languages. For example, if this statement is true, then do that. If the statement is not true, then there is need for the system to branch to a different set of procedures. Unfortunately, in many problems, the conditionality is so great that the number of paths grows explosively, often beyond the capabilities of the system (Rauch-Hindin 1986).

The first expert system on which I worked was for student aid and grants, so that the student could sit at a computer and determine whether or not the student's eligibility requirements were met. Unfortunately, this type of expert system only produced results that were consistent with the results produced by the expert, but the system only mimicked the rules the expert outlined. Since that time, now many years later, it is common to have a battery of expert systems that have been developed for many areas. In the **field of medicine**, there are **expert systems** available in numerous special fields such as antibiotics and infectious diseases, cancer, dermatology, family practice, gynecology, orthopedics, and numerous other fields (Med Exp Sys 2004).

One expert software system called **CLIPS (C Language Integrated Production System)** originated back in 1984 at NASA's Johnson Space Center. The artificial intelligence section at the center had developed over a dozen prototype expert-system applications. Out of these experiences, the prototype version of CLIPS was developed in 1985. CLIPS is now maintained independently as public domain software. (CLIPS FAQ 2004).

Doctor's Orders is an expert system, developed by individuals at Ohio State University (OSU) health systems that is on the leading edge of patient care organizations using computerized physician order entry (CPOE) systems which, authorities say, best represents the legacy of years of expert systems development work in health care. What OSU has accomplished, according to experts, is a microcosm of what will happen across health care in the next few years. Doctor's Orders, now in use for nearly two and a half years in a huge integrated health system with 2,000 physicians, 6,000 staff, 897 beds, and 40 care sites has 100 percent of the orders performed electronically with 80 percent physically entered by the physicians, and the rest are verbal orders entered by nurses but cosigned by physicians (Hagland 2003).

5GL-Doctor Personal Edition, from Australia, is described as an easy-to-use, friendly, and highly reliable, handheld expert system designed for self-diagnosis, containing four thousand symptoms and signs to generate the problem. A similar expert system, but more advanced, is available for use by professional medical personnel to assist in diagnosis (5GL Doctor 2004).

Intec Engineering began as a four-person organization in 1984 and demonstrates how an organization can begin with a willingness to share tacit knowledge and continue using this capability as the company grows. KM remained an indispensable function as the company acquired the various tools and techniques for sharing explicit knowledge. These all fell short when it came to tacit knowledge, and the organization had increased to around three thousand employees by the year 2000. A voluntary task force of engineers convened to explore knowledge management needs and to look at ways this growing company could address them. The main goal was to enable employees to find existing documents or locate an expert who could answer a question, or at least find out how to get an answer. The group decided to evaluate expertise location software and selected software from the AskMe Corporation, in part because the company could implement it without much modification. This resulted in an employee knowledge network, called **AskIntec**, and debuted on Intec's intranet in 2002. Employees all over the world now use the system to find information already on hand or to make connections with internal experts regarding a specific question. AskIntec is described as a fairly common system as there is only so much ingenuity involved in creating a system to pinpoint corporate knowledge. It has been the approach used from the start, a project management effort in a systematic way, with user feedback to gain employee involvement. The whole point of an employee knowledge network is to encourage people to participate because they are truly motivated to share their expertise. To encourage participation, Intec is attempting to make knowledge sharing a criterion in performance reviews. Intec now has seven hundred employees with three hundred to five hundred logging onto AskIntec weekly. The number using the system is impressive; however, the company needs to increase the number of employees who answer the questions (Santosus 2003).

David Skyrme describes what he calls the **three C's of knowledge sharing**: culture, co-opetition (a blend of cooperation and competition), and commitment. In the area of culture, as referenced above, sharing can be natural and a policy that has been going on for years. In other organizations, knowledge is power, even if it is held by only a few individuals who have sufficient knowledge by which to hold their peers to ransom. In many cases, Skyrme admits that knowledge is power, however, but it is typically not the primary reason for lack of knowledge sharing. He feels that the "not invented here" syndrome is a more common reason. People take pride in not having to seek advice from others and in wanting to discover new ways for themselves. Some individuals do not realize how useful particular knowledge is to others; knowledge deprived in one area may be a trigger for innovation—many innovative developments coming from knowledge connections across different disciplines and organizational boundaries. Lack of trust is a common item when an individual has shared knowledge that is then passed off as the idea of someone else. Lack of time is a reason given by many organizations plus the pressures on productivity, on deadlines, and the idea that the more knowledgeable you are, the more people are waiting to request you to work on the next task. Other barriers cited by experts include functional silos, individualism, poor means of knowledge capture, inadequate technology, internal competition, and top-down decision making. Generally, a mix of structural and infrastructure barriers are exacerbated by predominance of human ones—social, behavioral, and psychological (Skyrme 2002).

Some of the most helpful resources in the management of knowledge are portals. A "portal" is defined, according to *Webster's New World Computer Dictionary tenth edition*, as "a page on the Web that attempts to provide an attractive starting point for Web sessions. Typically included are links to breaking news, weather forecasts, stock quotes, free e-mail service, sports scores, and a subject guide to information available on the Web." A portal page may appear on an organization's Web site, on an **intranet,** or on an **extranet.** An "intranet" is defined from the same source in the above paragraph as "a computer network designed to meet the internal needs of a single organization or company that is based on Internet technology (TCP/IP). Not necessarily open to the external Internet and almost certainly not accessible from the outside, an intranet enables organizations to make internal resources available using familiar Internet clients, such as Web browsers, newsreaders, and e-mail." An "extranet" is described as "an intranet (internal TCP/IP network) that had been selectively opened to a firm's suppliers, customers, and strategic allies" (Webster 2003b).

Tom Kaneshige describes **Honeywell International,** a $24-billion technology and manufacturing leader, with offices and factories in ninety countries, as having the steps necessary to build a powerful knowledge network within its prized employee portal. The technology within Honeywell was the latest;

however, the culture of the human factor was the Achilles' heel because it had to be changed if the knowledge network was going to work. Honeywell's current culture could be traced back to its acquisition of Allied Signal in 1999. A year and a half later the **MyHoneywell** employee portal was launched as a means to consolidate some four hundred internal Web sites and standardize on a Sun Microsystems-Tibco platform serving up internal content, such as human resources information and corporate edicts, and external content from Yahoo. The portal used the typical design to provide an attractive starting point. MyHoneywell portal reached eighty thousand employees and cost between $1.25 million to $2.5 million. The decision to add a knowledge network was made in early 2002 with a miniengine inside the MyHoneywell that would lead employees to a searchable directory of experts throughout the company with the ability to ask questions and receive answers quickly. During this time Honeywell was going through the usual rounds of layoffs in a troubled economy that reduced the headcount from more than 120,000 to 108,000. As a result, employees kept largely to themselves with the "thinking going that my value is what's in my head and if I share it, maybe I will not be as valuable." It was not that people did not want to help others; they just helped those they trusted. The ideal result from the employee portal and the knowledge network was tribal sharing. Honeywell convinced many employees to open up and share their business tips, but there is still work ahead as many more employees need to access these tools. More than 30 percent of the 108,000 employees still do not have access to the basic employee portal, and only about 1,500 employees, mostly Honeywell's cross functional Six Sigma and Digitization groups, are on the knowledge network. It is intended that the knowledge network will reach twenty thousand to thirty thousand users. For every expansion effort, there is a cultural hurdle to overcome, such as the difficulty in knowledge sharing in Communist China. The knowledge network poses other unique concerns such as a salesperson at a public company, answering a question on the network that may accidentally reveal information about a big client to someone outside of sales, resulting in a confidentiality breach. In other words, there are all sorts of risks (Kanesshige 2003).

The best description of a large organization changing its culture is documented in the book *Who Says Elephants Can't Dance?* by **Louis V. Gerstner Jr.** When Gerstner took over at IBM, it had over $8 billion in debt and had cut seventy-three thousand jobs. At the time, the consensus appeared to be that the company should be broken up into independent smaller units. Gerstner's reaction to the breaking up was, "maybe yes, maybe no." The new boss flew to France to meet with the mightiest of the "IBM nobles", as he called them, who made up the EMBA, that stood for IBM Europe, Middle East, and Africa. One of the first things the new boss found was that the company was made up of powerful geographical fiefdoms with duplicate infrastructures in each country. Out of the ninety thousand EMBA employees, twenty-three thousand were in support functions (Gerstner 2002).

At Gerstner's first major press conference, his "coming-out party" as he put it, he informed the press that IBM did not need a new vision and that the number one priority was to restore the company to profitability. As he wrote, "**keeping IBM together** was the first strategic decision, and, I believe the most important decision I ever made—not just at IBM, but in my entire business career." A major task was breaking up the fiefdoms that ended up with the formation of IBM Global Services. Gerstner felt that IBM had only one $86 billion business and did not have multiple businesses. He only wanted a single class of knowledge workers. These steps were all involved in the cultural transformation that he described as the single and most difficult task, one that needed constant reinforcement because the company could yet again succumb to the arrogance of success (Gerstner 2002).

Along with changing the **IBM culture**, Gerstner changed the company from a product-based business to that of a services business. For example, an outsourcing contract for seven years might lose money the first year. This type of business was foreign for employees to understand and appreciate its significance. It included IBM's "e-business" in competition with such terms like the "information superhighway" and "e-commerce." This change in culture made it possible for IBM to develop and maintain the "single class of knowledge workers" that was referenced earlier. Without the culture change, the knowledge workers would not have developed into a single class (Gerstner 2002).

Although not really pertinent to the knowledge development subject, Gerstner's comments on the **information technology industry** need to be included. Without an IT technical background, he came to the job prepared to be challenged by the technology; unfortunately, he was totally unprepared for the characters and bizarre practices of the computer industry. Without including the names of the CEOs in his book, it is sufficient to say that he considered the industry to be a 24/7/365 three-ring circus having never witnessed any such behavior by individuals who are the most outspoken leaders he had ever met. He described, some, not all, as making outrageous remarks, attacking one another publicly with great relish and with no qualms about denigrating the other guy's products, promises, and pronouncements (Gerstner 2002). According to Ira Sager, "perhaps the biggest gap in an otherwise solid book is Gerstner's failure to take on his critics . . . and that Gerstner may not dish out the dirt like other tech CEOs, but his rich experience is worth more than any gossipy memoir" (Sager 2002).

Mr. Gerstner left IBM's culture so changed that it was ideal for the extension and further development of e-business in a knowledge management environment. IBM's purchase of **Lotus Development Corporation** when Gerstner was in charge was the result of a hostile takeover by IBM, its first, and at the time, the biggest software deal in history with a final price of $3.2 billion. Any software acquisition is risky because the real asset you are acquiring is human. If the people decide to quit, all you have left are some buildings, office equipment, and access to a customer-installed base. IBM's effort to win over the Lotus workforce that had an Internet-centric culture, including the crown jewel, a product called Notes, and all the employees who made it possible made the acquisition a winner (Gerstner 2002).

During November 2002, IBM CEO Sam Palmisano used the phrase **e-business on demand** to describe a radically new future for organizational computing. This was a sweeping vision, but one ideal for IBM, a company with wide-flung resources in research, business and technical consulting, software innovation and hardware. Since its introduction, the industry has watched as the ambitious vision attempts to become a reality. IBM Lotus Workplace software has a unique role in the implementation of that vision. Business on demand is defined by IBM as a technological state of business in which business processes—processes that involve not only employees but suppliers, partners, and even customers—can respond with speed to any market opportunity, customer demand, or external threat. The IBM Lotus Workplace role is one of integrating collaboration by taking all of Lotus's collaborative products, including decades of investment in messaging, e-learning and scheduling, awareness, e-meetings, team rooms, workflows, and making them assessable through a single role-based portal where they can be integrated with each other and with other applications and used in context with the task at hand (IBM Lotus Workplace 2003). Although Gerstner had changed IBM from a product company to a services company, during the period since November 2002, referenced above, the company, and in particular **Sam Palmisano**, had faced a number of outside events that slowed the gains and expansions desired. According to David Kirkpatrick's article "Inside Sam's $100 Billion Growth Machine" in the June 24, 2004, *Fortune,* the two huge goals, to get this giant growing again and to return IBM to greatness, are progressing even better than expected (Kirkpatrick 2004b). Since the June article, IBM posted a 17 percent increase in earnings during the second quarter of 2004, with the services business, which accounts for half its revenue, growing 6.5 percent during the quarter (Kirkpatrick 2004b; Bulkeley 2004b).

"Technologists never evangelize without a **disclaimer**: 'Technology is just an enabler.' True enough—and the disclaimer discloses part of the problem: Enabling what? One flaw in knowledge management is that it often neglects to ask what knowledge to manage and toward what end. Knowledge management activities are all over the map. Building databases, measuring intellectual capital, establishing corporate libraries, building intranets, sharing best practices, installing groupware, leading training programs, leading cultural change, fostering collaboration, creating virtual organizations—all of these are knowledge management, and every functional and staff leader can lay claim to it. But no one claims the big question: Why?" (Hawthorne n.d.; Stewart 2002).

Tom Stewart's disclaimer does not stand alone as industry case studies provide illustrative examples of successes and failures in integrating knowledge management technologies for enabling organizational business processes and new business models. Based upon insights from selected case studies, an article by Dr.Yogesh Malotra identifies three key paradigms that have characterized the implementation of KM systems, technologies, and techniques in organizational business processes. The first of three is the "inputs-driven paradigm" that considers information technology and KM as synonymous. This paradigm has its primary focuses on technologies such as digital repositories, databases, intranets, and groupware systems that have been the mainstay of many KM implementation projects. The choices of the technologies are what drive the KM equations with primary emphasis on getting the right information. The second is the processing-driven paradigm of KM that has its focus on best practices, training and learning programs, cultural change, collaboration, and virtual organizations. KM in this case is considered primarily as a means of processing information for various business activities. The majority of the proponents of **RTE (real time enterprises)** belong to this paradigm given their credo of getting the right information to the right person at the right time. Unfortunately, technology is often depicted as an easy solution to achieve many types of information processing; however, there are implementation failures often caused by cost and time overruns that make large-scale technology projects fail. The third is the outcome-driven paradigm of KM that has its primary focus on business performance. These three paradigms are making preparations for the coming of the real time enterprise, called the **new knowledge management**, where the premise is to get the right knowledge to the right people at the right time in real time (Malhotra 2003).

One of the most highly recognized organizations for having an excellent knowledge program is **Buckman Laboratories**. The company started with four workers in 1945 and now is a global organization with over 1,300 employees in over 70 countries. There is a willingness to share how knowledge is treated and shared within the company and around the world. Mr. Buckman stated that Buckman Laboratories never used the term "knowledge management" because the thinking within the organization was that it was the wrong term to describe what they did and what they should be focused on as individuals and as organizations. If you want to create value out of this stuff called knowledge, he felt that if you are going to manage knowledge, then you would only be managing about 10 percent or that knowledge that was written down (or explicit knowledge). Since you can not manage the 90 percent (tacit knowledge) that is in heads of the employees, they did not use the term. He explained that if they wanted to create value as an individual or as an organization, they had to get the tacit knowledge in each 'Community of One' to move to another 'Community of One' and on to a 'Community around issues' or a 'Community of Practice' or the organization as a whole. He also stated that the only way to create value is through the movement of knowledge. Knowledge that does not move creates no value, either for the individual that possesses it or for the rest of the organization. An individual will have no power unless value is created and this is done by moving away from hoarding knowledge and to gaining power by sharing knowledge. This is the reason that Buckman Laboratories has always been focused on 'Knowledge Sharing'. The system for sharing tacit knowledge across the organization was established and built on the needs of the organization (Buckman 2003).

In spite of the lack of use of the "knowledge management" term at Buckman Laboratories, the lady who was CIO at Buckman is also the author of a best-selling book *The Complete Idiot's Guide to Knowledge Management*. As an author, **Dr. Melissie Clemmons Rumizen** acknowledges that every organization is different and that no one approach works for everyone; and even with the help of her book, it will take some creativity on the user or reader's part to obtain the desired results (Rumizen 2002).

In the foreword of the Rumizen book, **Lawrence Prusak** recognizes the author's ability to provide a solid review of the knowledge-based ideas and practices that have influenced how companies function in the knowledge management area. She does this by focusing on common-sense principles and covering a wide range of topics ranging from how to work with information technology to the fine points of a communications strategy. Organizational culture is one of the most important topics along with the ability to manage change. Also included is the fact that leading a knowledge management effort in an organization is sometimes a thankless job requiring a jack-of-all-trades background (Prusak 2002; Rumizen 2002).

The importance of knowledge had finally been recognized by business and other organization leaders making it all the more necessary to determine how knowledge should be managed and what information technology (IT) tools should be selected to support the knowledge management effort. As the complexities of knowledge management have increased in recent years and the variety of IT solutions are improving in every area, executives have an ever-increasing challenge in deciding what combinations should be chosen. According to an article in a recent *Communications of the ACM*, there are two basic approaches for which IT can provide support: codification and personalization. With codification, more explicit and structured knowledge is codified and stored in knowledge bases, electronic knowledge repositories. Direct, personalized communications provides for more tacit and unstructured knowledge to be exchanged or shared. The article describes twelve organizations selected from the twenty winners of the **Most Admired Knowledge Enterprises (MAKE) 2002** award shown in the following Web site: *http://www.knowledgebusiness. com/uploads/2002_Global_MAKE_Summary.pdf.* The organizations in the article were classified along two dimensions (product based versus service based and high-versus low-volatility context). Of the twelve organizations selected, seven were product based; three in low-volatility context: British Petroleum, Buckman Laboratories, and Shell; with four in high-volatility context: Hewlett-Packard, Microsoft, Siemens Technologies, and Xerox. Of the five classified as service based, Ernst and Young, KPMG, and Siemens Business Services were low-volatility context with McKinsey and Skandia in high-volatility context. In conclusion, all organizations were apparently operating well-organized knowledge-management functions; however, each depended on whether the organization was product based or service based and whether the company operated in a high- or low-volatility context causing the organization to have distinct patterns in their approaches to knowledge management strategies and the information technology support provided (Kankanhalli 2003).

A more detailed description of knowledge management in a much larger number of organizations are found in *Leading with Knowledge Management Practices in Global Infotech Companies* (Rao 2003). Editor Rao provides another definition of knowledge management. "Knowledge management can be defined as a systematic discipline and a set of approaches to enable information and knowledge to grow, flow, and create value in an organization: this involves people, information, workflows, best practices, alliances, and communities of practice." The book is described as being one of the case studies and stories about the design and implementation of KM. The editor contacted knowledge management professionals in the information technology sector from around the world to solicit the story of their KM practices based on parameters like evolutionary trends, infrastructure, knowledge assets, communities of practice, return on investment, cultural issues, capacity building, and incentive schemes. Out of the group, fifteen organizations agreed to permit the inclusion of full-length narratives that are contained in separate chapters, making up the bulk of the book. Other individuals responded to brief questionnaires, which are also summed up in the text. In addition, interviews were conducted with KM analysts at IDC, Gartner, and APQC, and some of their findings have also been included. Organizations included are: EDS, EMC, Fujitsu Consulting, Hughes Software Systems, i2, IBM, i-flex, Infosys Technologies, Inktomi, JD Edwards, MITRE, Novell, Open Text, Oracle, SAS, PMC-Sierra, Sun Microsystems, Philippines, and Xerox (Rao 2003).

From my knowledge management research, it appears that most organizations have found a way to manage **explicit knowledge** so that there is some form of documentation and/or inventory. As described previously, **tacit knowledge** management is a different form of management because the tacit knowledge is in people's heads and may not be formed yet, just the beginning of an idea or concept. A large number of organizations have developed a method to function with the tacit knowledge that has been identified within the organization; much of it has been identified with individuals who are recognized as the most knowledgeable in that area. Some individuals do not like to be identified as the most knowledgeable. This may be due to the culture of the organization and the way it seems to control the individuals' willingness to share what tacit knowledge they have.

Hundreds of **tacit knowledge software** packages are on the market. The word "tacit" can be confusing because some packages are designed for use in optimization of existing applications such as performance bottlenecks. Others are designed for use in the review of source code in the context of the system on which it resides. To be more specific, *KMWorld Magazine* recognized The Brain Technologies Corporation's BrainEKP (enterprise knowledge platform) as a trend-setting product of 2003 for its usability, adopt rate, and total cost of ownership. According to the editor in chief of *KMWorld* this software product was recognized for having been designed with the user in mind, reducing the level of expertise and programming required for their offerings to deliver peak performance. He described the software as an excellent example of a solution that users can easily update and maintain. It includes drag-and-drop authoring features that provide a powerful method of collaboration and knowledge sharing for companies that need to share complex sets of information online instantly without the need for any IT assistance. The enterprise knowledge platform is designed not only to help companies find information faster but to capture and present information the way people naturally think about it—in context of all related issues and topics. The **BrainEKP** enables users to create multiple views of information for divergent user groups and to extend thinking and business processes across multiple data sources and applications. A complete platform is the solution for information sharing and collaboration. In addition to the significant industry recognition gained by BrainEKP as a trend-setting product of 2003, BrainEKP has also been named 2003 Product of the Year by *Call Center Magazine* (BrainEKP 2003).

Now we will examine a British tacit knowledge management system called **Mint MCI (managing collective intelligence).** According to the developer, Mint Business Solutions, the package provides an intranet and extranet collaboration and tacit knowledge management system. The software is designed to answer the question, "Are you capturing the full body of knowledge relating to a given subject?" Whether for customers, suppliers, markets, products, solutions, etc., what might make a complete knowledge set? It could include both tacit and explicit knowledge assets. MCI is designed to capture tacit knowledge, both in terms of nuggets and giving narrative context to explicit resources. Tacit knowledge has been defined as experiential knowledge based on clues, hunches, instinct, and personal insights—as distinct from formal, explicit knowledge. MCI seeks to provide a tool for the contribution and sharing of such typically undeclared knowledge. It provides an electronic medium for users to write; in turn the written contributions can be supported by further signposts or links to more explicit resources (or people) and/or provide context to the utilization of these resources. MCI is also a forum for the collaboration that can lead to decisions, solutions, best practice, and innovation (Mint 2003).

The Tacit Knowledge Systems Inc. based in Palo Alto, California, describes how one of its customers, Eastman Kodak Company, uses its **Tacit KnowledgeMail** software to automatically, discover the activity and expertise of people in its commercial and government systems (C&GS) unit and to help project teams coordinate development activities and build international networks. After the activity and expertise of people in the organization are identified, the software can connect them in real time to improve enterprise coordination and productivity (Tacit K 2002).

These examples of **tacit knowledge management software** seem sufficient to demonstrate that, in spite of the problems, there are major efforts in tacit software development and in their application. Of great importance in the tacit area is the need to be able to identity individuals who have the tacit knowledge, make it possible for them to locate each other, and provide communications for the exchange of tacit knowledge.

A hot topic in today's knowledge management area is the difference between managing content and managing knowledge. **Content management** focuses on information about a company, rather than about its customers. The extensive availability of the Internet enables companies to share information about themselves with more employees and customers than ever. Just as knowledge management expands its scope, so too does the need to impose uniformity on how, when, and to whom this information becomes available. Content management is the process of tracking and communicating all stages of editorial production. It is easy to automate because it comprises a repeatable sequence of tasks. However, content management is not really about content, but about what is happening with content. A software package called KnowledgeBase Enterprise Edition 3.0 from KnowledgeBase Solutions in Los Angeles, California, demonstrates the growing trend toward intertwining content management with knowledge management. According to Joe Fleischer's description, the software provides various ways to display knowledge-based items, such as lists of answers to frequently asked questions (FAQs), drill-down menus, glossaries, or collections of documents (Fleischer 2003).

On the **negative side of the content** discussion, **Jupitermedia** *http://www. internet.com/corporate/directions.html* released a report in February 2003 entitled "Why Content Management Software Hasn't Worked." It is a harsh report that states as a major reason for the software not working was that it was badly designed and massively overhyped. The report also claims that software companies lied about their products, charging criminal prices. A main reason for it not working was that organizations did not understand content. Users were after a quick fix and issued specifications that bore little relation to what they actually needed. However, the report goes on to point out that the software by not working did not mean that it can not work, and goes on to state what purchasers of content software need to do to become successful. At the head of the list is for users to specify what they need, not what they want. Users must stop thinking that they are entitled to special benefits when standardized solutions can deliver much faster, cheaper, and much more satisfactory results (McGovern 2003).

Another hot topic is knowledge management versus **document management (DM)**. According to some reports, a number of document management software vendors label their solutions as knowledge management (KM). We need to look at why DM is not KM. The systems in support of knowledge management are designed to channel information and knowledge to the most useful points within the organization. Internet-based systems when integrated with legacy information systems and financial control systems basically become a document management problem. Transacting business with virtual documents is what enables e-commerce to take place. The Internet is fundamentally a network of intelligent documents. Documents do not necessarily imply paper as they can be in CD-ROM format, a video segment, a hologram, or Web image. Documents of the future, whether as promotional mailings or on the Internet, will increasingly address the demands of the recipient. The difference between knowledge management and document management is the difference between technology and culture. Even though they are different concepts, they are working together to support modern organizations in improving business operations. In spite of the increasing momentum of the digital age, much of an organization's original materials and output remain in a paper-based format. Crucial to knowledge management is the ability to manage the creation, capture, route, search, and use—"in fact the whole life cycle of this material"—in support of the organization as a whole. There is an increasing need for DM and KM to work together in support of each other (KMFeature 2000).

A leading platform for document management and collaboration is **Open Text's Livelink** from Livelink Corporation. The company's intranet OLLIE hosts the global knowledge library and three communities of practice: competitive intelligence forum, customer dashboard, and knowledge centre. The company has had an extranet in operation since 1997 to improve collaboration with its affinity partners, participates in industry KM initiatives like APQC (American

Productivity & Quality Center), and has a Knowledge Management Advisory Board consisting of representatives from about twenty of its top customers (Open Text's Livelink 2003).

The following view of **KM in Europe** is included to equalize the discussion. The European countries have recognized the importance of the knowledge economy. However, there are different levels of knowledge activities concerning EU members and non-member states. The European Council has set a goal for 2010: to become the most competitive and dynamic knowledge-based economy in the world. Eastern European nations can learn during their early stages from the evolution of KM in more developed countries. According to Leif Edvinsson (the world's first director of intellectual capital at Skandia, and today CEO of Unic) the Scandinavian countries pioneered the knowledge economy. Mariusz Strojny (KM coordinator at KPMG) highlights the fact that Europe is more advanced with KM than the US. This is mostly because US companies concentrate more on technology than on the cultural and social aspects of KM. Workforce cultures and characteristics in Europe can have a positive as well as a negative influence on KM's evolution. Much work and practice on KM is coming from non-profit organizations, the public sector, and not only from large-scale companies as it used to be. Besides EU countries, the non-member states are making progress with their own initiatives. However, it is still not common practice and more developed nations are seen as benchmarks. There are still certain problems from the Communist period and a lack of collaboration between institutions in the non EU countries (Edvinsson 2003).

When the United States turned over the entire canal system to the **Republic of Panama** at the end of 1999, the many military bases and installations amounted to nearly five thousand buildings and one hundred thousand acres of land. Among the many plans for the use of the military bases was an ambitious project for the development of a proposed City of Knowledge, Panama Canal Zone, a sprawling international university and research complex (Woodard 1997).

The **City of Knowledge** is a success story, not completed by any means. Even so, the idea is being fulfilled. The vacant military housing is being rented to technological and research companies to form a synergy of progressive commercial and scholastic activity. In 2003, the author, Michael Manville, described her visit with a group of McGill University students who were studying environmental sciences and sustainable development in the City of Knowledge. Their housing area had excellent facilities resulting from the United States' adequately funded military housing and support facilities such as an Olympic-sized swimming pool, playing fields, Internet connection, a cafeteria, and a church all within walking distance of the residential area. The residences were spacious and complete with hot water, household appliances, and even hardwood floors. The International Tecnoparque in the City of Knowledge has already attracted more than forty companies with offices in the complex. Companies have to complete an admission application explaining the kind of business they plan to conduct and what kind of research or technical expertise they intend to contribute. Company applications are put before the admissions committee before being accepted. The goal of the tecnoparque is to provide an encouraging environment for innovations in information technology, biological science, and multimodal transportation (Manville 2003).

CORE KNOWLEDGE AND EDUCATION STANDARDS

PROFESSOR E. D. **Hirsch Jr**. pointed out in his 1987 book, *Cultural Literacy*, that the single most disastrous mistake of American schooling during the past forty years had been the misguided emphasis on skills. Professor Hirsch believed in the fundamental psychological principle that knowledge builds on knowledge—that we learn something new by building on what we already know. Not many years ago, it was common to identify a student's level of knowledge with grade completion. For example, the completion of a specific grade generally ensured that the student knew certain multiplication tables. The influx of calculators may have erased this level of understanding; however, there was need for an accepted level of knowledge to be associated with grade level completion. Recognizing this need, Professor Hirsch built on his cultural literacy concept and founded the **Core Knowledge Foundation** in Charlottesville, Virginia, in 1986. The objective of this effort was to make available the tools designed to provide elementary school children with a core of knowledge at each grade level. The core knowledge concept advocates the teaching of a carefully sequenced body of knowledge in a broad range of subject areas. This concept became the core knowledge sequence when developed in 1990; field-tested at Three Oaks Elementary in Fort Myers, Florida; revised in 1992; and updated in 1993. The concept is being used in 2004 in over six hundred core knowledge elementary schools across the country (Core Knowledge 2004).

Core knowledge goes to the heart of a fundamental need in public education. If all children are to be given a fair chance to make steady academic progress, then we need to ensure that each student who enters a class at the beginning of the year is ready to gain the new knowledge and skills to be taught in the coming year. When teachers do not know what children in the same grade level in other classrooms are learning much less in earlier and later grades, they cannot reliably predict that children will come to class prepared with a shared core of knowledge and skills. For a school to be successful, teachers need a **common vision** of what they want their students to know and be able to accomplish. They need to have clear, specific learning goals, as well as the sense of mutual accountability that comes from shared commitment to helping all children achieve those goals (Holden and Hirsch 1996).

The **Goals 2000: Educate America Act,** enacted in 1994, apparently ignored the work of Professor Hirsch and his Core Knowledge Foundation. The act provided eight national education goals to be completed by the year 2000. The act established in the executive branch a **national education goals panel** to be composed of eighteen members, with duties in general to report to the president, the secretary (of education), and the Congress regarding the progress of the nation and the states are making toward achieving the national education goals; to report on state opportunity-to-learn standards and strategies; and submit to the president nominations for appointment to the **National Education Standards and Improvement Council.** Also established in the executive branch, the council was composed of nineteen members with duties including the identity of areas in which voluntary national content standards need to be developed; to certify voluntary national content standards and voluntary national student performance standards; forward such voluntary national content standards and voluntary national student performance standards to the goals panel for review; and develop a process for periodically reviewing any voluntary national content standards, voluntary national student performance standards, and voluntary national opportunity-to-learn standards that have been certified (Goals 2000).

In a 1996 Goals 2000 progress report the answer to "**what is a standard?**" was given as "academic standards describe what every student should know and be able to do in core academic content areas. They also define how students demonstrate their skills and knowledge" (Standard 1996).

By 1998, Goals 2000 was implementing **standards-based reform** by focusing on ensuring that all children meet high academic standards. "This emphasis on result is embodied in changes in instructional and institutional systems—curriculum and instruction, professional development, assessment and accountability, school and leadership organization, and parental and community involvement—that are aligned to content and performance standards. Because Goals 2000 represents the effective implementation of standards-based reform, the two are inextricably linked. Therefore, the success of Goals 2000 must be tied to state progress in implementing standards-based reform and its respective elements" (Standards-Based Reform 1998).

The national education goals panel was dissolved pursuant to congressional mandate. Its Web site remained functionally operational, but last updated on March 6, 2002 (NEGP 2002).

The **Education Sciences Reform Act of 2002** established the **Institute of Education Sciences (IES)** as the research arm of the Department of Education. The mission of the institute is to expand knowledge and provide information on the condition of education, practices that improve academic achievement, and the effectiveness of federal and other education programs. The institute's goal is the transformation of education into an evidence-based field in which decision makers routinely seek out the best available research and data before adopting programs or practices that will affect significant numbers of students. The director was appointed to a six-year term in November 2002. There are three centers: the National Center for Education Statistics, the National Center for Education Research, and the National Center for Education Evaluation and Regional Assistance (IES 2004).

In addition to the three centers described above under the supervision of the Institute of Education Sciences, there are ten **regional educational laboratories** that are educational research and development organizations supported by contracts with the institute. These laboratories support the states that make them up. For example, Kansas is one of seven states in the central region called McREL. The other states are Colorado, Missouri, Nebraska, North Dakota, South Dakota, and Wyoming. Each laboratory has a designated specialty. McREL's specialty is national leadership area: standards-based educational practice (REL 2004).

I was amazed to learn how much research has been accomplished since the formation of the IES and the ten regional laboratories. Even more amazing is the organization of the research completed for use by anyone with access to the Internet. Using the McREL laboratory as an example, its Web site is *www.mcrel.org* with publication lists available by looking through "McREL by Topic." Virtually every listed publication was either produced directly through the regional laboratory contract or is a spin-off or scale-up of that work. There is a regional laboratory Web site, *http://www.relnet.org*, that provides a review of the work of the network in general, with links to the Web sites of the individual laboratories to view specific information about their reports and other work (Brannan 2004).

In 2004, the **U.S. Department of Education (ED)** provided about $36 billion to states and school districts, primarily through formula-based grant programs, to improve elementary and secondary schools and meet the special needs of students. To help strengthen teaching and learning in colleges and other postsecondary institutions, ED is providing about $2.5 billion and about $3.3 billion to support rehabilitation, research and development, statistics, and assessment (Overview 2004).

WISDOM

WISDOM IS THE ability to apply previously obtained knowledge to solve a problem or develop a solution. It is hard to comprehend the amount of information written since the time of Socrates, Plato, Aristotle, and many others including books of the Bible and in particular the book of Proverbs which is devoted to wisdom. In spite of all the study, we are asking the same questions about wisdom inquired of these pioneers many centuries ago. Ideally, it would be useful to provide a historical background of these many writings; however, the volume of the material precludes any attempt of this effort on my part. Three references are recommended for those who have a need for more detailed study: *Wisdom: Its Nature, Origins, and Development* by Robert J. Sternberg (Sternberg 1990); *The Story of Philosophy* by Will Durant (Durant 1961); and *Philosophy for Dummies* by Tom Morris (Morris 1999).

Beyond the previous discussions of knowledge management, the goal for each person, organization, and government is wisdom. So what is wisdom? Here are some additional definitions:

Wisdom is the ability to make sound choices and the best decisions. Wisdom is intelligence shaped with experience, information softened by understanding. Wisdom is not something with which a person is born. Intelligence is. Cleverness is, but wisdom is not. Wisdom only comes from living, from making mistakes or from learning from others who have made mistakes. Today, wisdom is one of those slightly old-fashioned words, the type that slip out of style because they sound less punchy than the jargon we start using in their place. In time, we forget about using the word at all. Instead of using wisdom, we talk about cleverness, IQ, managerial know-how, or use one of the fifty not-quite-synonymous words. None of those really are interchangeable with wisdom; they are used instead. Meanwhile, wisdom, the original concept, is forgotten (Pino 2003).

Wisdom requires knowledge management, organizing it for the best use. Russell Ackoff, a systems theorist, described the need for understanding to take place between the acquisition of knowledge and wisdom as a very necessary process, one that is cognitive and analytical. It is a process by which knowledge can be used when new knowledge is synthesized from previously held knowledge. Other authors state that the difference between understanding and knowledge is the difference between "learning" and "memorizing." Individuals who have understanding can undertake useful actions because they can synthesize new knowledge, or in some cases, at least new information, from what is previously known (and understood). Artificial intelligence systems possess understanding in the sense that they are able to synthesize new knowledge from previously stored information and knowledge. The authors do not believe that understanding is a separate level of its own as used by Ackoff but that understanding supports the transition from data to information to knowledge to wisdom. This is also a process by which we discern, or judge, between right and wrong, good and bad. Wisdom is also described as a uniquely human state—that wisdom requires one to have a soul—for it resides as much in the heart as in the mind (Bellinger 2004).

To many people wisdom has become indistinguishable from knowledge. However, they are different things and that which is often indicated to be wisdom is simply opinion. **Knowledge is not wisdom** because wisdom is the proper use of knowledge. The glut of information that continues to increase may add to our knowledge, but it can block our development of wisdom due to our being so busy trying to process more and more information; we do not have time for the quiet contemplation that is essential for the development of wisdom. It is essential to let the unwanted information go in one ear and out the other. Knowledge is a peculiar thing because it can deceive us into thinking we are wise. To repeat, knowledge is not wisdom. This is demonstrated with individuals who may have many degrees and appear to be incredibly smart, yet their life is a struggle, one upset after another, because they lack wisdom having failed to learn to apply the knowledge they have (Foundations 2004).

Knowledge that does not take shape in deeds, that does not apply itself to life, is trivia. If **knowledge is not applied,** it is just knowledge for knowledge's sake, just something to get intellectual about and may lead to arrogance. Knowledge by itself does not result in clear vision, a proper perspective, meaning, and the right behavior. When this transformation does occur, we call it wisdom. But how do we get wisdom, develop it, and make it a part of our lives? Basically, it is important to understand that wisdom is grounded in reality in two ways. We need to learn to be aware of ourselves and those around us in order to learn from other peoples' successes and from their mistakes. Second, you are being disconnected from reality when you know something works, and you do not do it. We can justify doing things in the same old way, but we are only kidding ourselves when we fail to make changes that should be obvious. Living with reality takes exertion on our part; however, it is crucial that we do the things that we know must be done and refrain from doing those things we know should not be done. Stated another way, in order to attain wisdom we must understand the law of cause and effect. Up to a given point, we are the results of all the decisions we have made and the actions we have taken. When a mistake is made, evaluate what action or actions were taken and attempt to determine why the outcome was not desirable. Make every effort to make changes in the solution used previously and obtain a more successful outcome. After all, life is made up of a series of course corrections that add up to the substance of your life. In order to live by wisdom and principle, the individual must remove the personalities involved, the emotions and egos, in order to do the right thing. After your decision as to the proper course of action, the personalities may be put back in, and you can proceed with what really needs to be done. In order to carry out and articulate each situation, one must be proactive, not more assertive, but using an attitude that is the product of one's thinking that comes from being connected to one's own behavior. Having a long term perspective, seeing the big picture, is a foundation principle of wisdom to look beyond the immediate situation. Wisdom helps us develop emotional maturity by placing us in our proper roles in relationship with everything else around us. Wisdom requires humility and infers that as an individual you must be teachable. As an individual, you are the only one that can gain wisdom for yourself. It is up to you, as no one can make you wise or make you unwise. Philosophers are lovers of wisdom, and we should all be philosophers (Foundations 2004).

Who are these **philosophers** to whom we are indebted? Starting with Plato, they gave us definitions of wisdom and, as good philosophers, they are not satisfied until they explored the furthest depths of the question they are asking. As a result, philosophers are known as deep thinkers. Quite often, when philosophical ideas are difficult to understand, it is not that they are too abstract, or too far removed from our everyday life, but that they are too concrete. Many do not have the patience to study the in-depth requirements that give philosophers their rightful advantage over those who refuse to study and consider all facets of a statement or problem. Occasionally, philosophy touches so deeply on familiar things that we fail to understand because the subject is too close to home. The next question is "what is philosophy?" It is defined in *Encarta* as "examination of basic concepts, the branch of knowledge or academic study devoted to the systematic examination of basic concepts such as truth, existence, reality, causality, and freedom." Philosophy actually begins with the recognition of ignorance; however, an introductory course typically begins with a study of metaphysics to teach the difference between what we can and can not know. Then the study of logic to teach the difference between what words mean when they refer to something we can know about, and what they mean when they refer to something of which we are necessarily ignorant. Once this theoretical foundation is reached to build on, our new understanding can be applied in practical ways. This is accomplished by reaching out for the truth and knowledge which is relevant to human life, and this search for a "true science," **philosophy**, is properly called the love of wisdom. Through loving wisdom, we can enter into the fourth stage of the philosophical task without being "lost in wonderland," so to speak. For the final task is to learn truly to appreciate the wonder of silence. To some degree, all philosophy begins and ends with silent wonder.

I like this paragraph written by Joseph W. Meeker and taken from his article **"Wisdom and Wilderness"**:

"Wisdom is a state of the human mind characterized by profound understanding and deep insight. It is often, but not necessarily, accompanied by extensive formal knowledge. Unschooled people can acquire wisdom, and wise people can be found among carpenters, fishermen, or housewives. Wherever it exists, wisdom shows itself as a perception of the relativity and relationships among things. It is an awareness of wholeness that does not lose sight of particularity or concreteness, or of intricacies of interrelationships. It is where left and right brains come together in a union of logic and poetry and sensation, and where self-awareness is no longer at odds with awareness of the otherness of the world. Wisdom cannot be confined to a specialized field, nor is it an academic discipline; it is the consciousness of wholeness and integrity that transcends both. Wisdom is complexity understood and relationships accepted" (Meeker 2003).

Joe Firestone and Mark McElroy have developed what they call **the new knowledge management (TNKM)** using a **complex adaptive systems approach (CAS)** that provides for personal knowledge different from interpersonal systems, and enterprise systems. In this development, they have defined knowledge as "an encoded, tested and evaluated, and surviving structure of information that helps the system that created it to adapt. Knowledge Processing refers to the interrelated activities that produce such a structure of information" (Firestone 2004). Although I admire their work and contributions, for the present, I prefer to keep it simple and use **personal knowledge development (PKD). Individual knowledge management (IKM) or personal knowledge management (PKM) may also be used; however, PKD is preferred.**

An example of the advancing technology support for individual knowledge management is a software package called **MailTack** that originated from European Union-sponsored research. MailTack is a stand-alone software tool being used to understand and support user behavior in complex e-mail discussions with the aim of contributing to systematic individual knowledge management applications. MailTack, based on a constructivist understanding of knowing, was developed as a tool for persistent business discussions combined with an individual knowledge assessment. The intent is to help the involved individuals in improving the effectiveness and efficiency of their asynchronous conversations. It is believed that MailTack contributes to make collaborative learning and asynchronous interaction (for cooperating, coaching, tutoring, etc.) more successful and attractive thus facilitating the dynamics of communities of practice and more generally learning communities (Bettoni 2002).

X1 software is another example of the advancing technology. It can search e-mail files created by Microsoft's Outlook Express, Netscape, and Eudora and search for words in e-mail attachments, words stored on the hard disk in word processing documents, spreadsheets, slide presentations, graphics, and database files (Mossberg 2004a).

Google Incorporated's first post-IPO maneuver was the release of free software that enables consumers to search e-mail and files saved in their computers. The software is called **Google Desktop Search** and available at *http://desktop.google.com*. Users can search within Microsoft Office and text files on their hard drives (Delaney 2004).

One of the most outstanding advancements to provide insight into data is **OLAP,** defined as "online analytical processing"; however, to some, it is not a definition; it is not even a clear description of what OLAP means. The term gives no indication of why you would want to use an OLAP tool, or even what an OLAP tool actually does. In addition, the term gives you no help in deciding if a product is an OLAP tool or not (Report 2003).

Before going into the **OLAP report** that supports the above paragraph, we should look at how OLAP has been explained by others. It is seen as a category of software technology that enables analysts, managers, and executives to gain insight into data through fast, consistent, interactive access to a wide variety of possible views of information that has been transformed from raw data to reflect the real dimensionality of the enterprise as understood by the user. Functionality-wise, OLAP is characterized by dynamic multidimensional analysis of consolidated enterprise data supporting end-user analytical and navigational activities including calculations and modeling applied across dimensions, through hierarchies and/or across members; trend analysis over sequential time periods; slicing subsets for on-screen viewing; drilling down to deeper levels of consolidation; reaching through to underlying detail data; and rotation to new dimensional comparisons in the viewing area. A multiuser client-server mode is used to implement OLAP and offers consistently rapid response to queries, regardless of database size and complexity. The user uses OLAP to help synthesize enterprise information through analysis of historical and projected data in various what-if data model scenarios. This is achieved through the server, referred to above, a high-capacity, multiuser data manipulation engine specifically designed to support and operate on multidimensional data structures. A multidimensional structure is arranged so that every data item is located and accessed based on the intersection of the dimension members which define that item. The server design and the structure of the data are optimized for rapid ad-hoc information retrieval in any orientation, as well as for fast, flexible calculation and transformation of raw data based on formulaic relationships. A more detailed description of the OLAP server shows that it may either physically stage the processed multidimensional information to deliver consistent and rapid response time to end users, or it may populate its data structures in real time from relational databases, or offer a choice of both. Using the current state of technology and the end user requirement for consistent and rapid response time, staging the multidimensional data in the OLAP server is often the preferred method (OLAP 2003).

Now let us return to the OLAP report. The report has been prepared and is updated with the view of using it to evaluate OLAP products and determine whether or not they meet the report's requirement for it to be recognized as an approved OLAP product. The definition included in the report is designed to be short and easy to remember using just five key words: **fast-analysis of shared multidimensional information or FASMI** for short. Since 1995, this definition has been used without any need for revision and now is widely adopted and cited in over 120 Web sites in about 30 countries. **"Fast"** means that the system is targeted to deliver most responses to users within about five seconds, with the simplest analyses taking no more than one second and very few taking more than twenty seconds. Independent research in the Netherlands has shown that end users assume that a process has failed if results are not received within thirty seconds, and they are apt to hit "Crl+Alt+Delete" unless the system warns them that the report will take longer. **"Analysis"** means that the system can cope with any business logic and statistical analysis that is relevant for the application and the user and keep it easy enough for the target user. Some preprogramming may be needed; we do not think it acceptable if all application definitions have to be done using a professional 4GL. It is necessary to allow the user to define new ad-hoc calculations as part of the analysis and to report on the data in any desired way, without having to program, so the report excludes products that do not allow adequate end user-oriented-calculation flexibility. **"Shared"** means that the system implements all the security requirements for confidentiality (possibly down to cell level) and, if multiple write access is needed, concurrent update locking at an appropriate level. **"Multidimensional"** is the key requirement in the definition used in the OLAP report. If a one word definition had to be selected, "multidimensional" would be the word. This view of the data includes full support for hierarchies and multiple hierarchies, as this is certainly the most logical way to analyze businesses and organizations. No underlying database technology is specified providing that the user gets a truly multidimensional conceptual view. **"Information"** includes all the data and derived information needed wherever it is and however much is relevant for the application. There is great variance in the different OLAP products and the amount of information they can handle. The largest OLAP product can hold at least a thousand times as much data as the smallest. This variety will add to their increased use (Report 2003).

In addition to the OLAP type of software, many organizations are finding it beneficial to share **business intelligence (BI)** capabilities in addition to top executives by including business partners, customers, and employees. A common way of sharing is through the use of executive **dashboards**, a.k.a. manager dashboards, executive cockpits, digital cockpits, or what was originally called executive information systems. A dashboard is really an intranet for a select group of users. Companies are finding that it is much better to permit employees to make immediate decisions in response to an opportunity than to force them to wait for some executive to be alerted to the opportunity and then make the decision. The dashboard supports the employee or executive by doing three things: (1) It answers fundamental questions about the business or business unit. (2) It alerts the user to issues or problems in such areas as production, sales, and revenue. (3) It helps make decisions that impact the business (Kirkland 2004).

The domain of statisticians and corporate analysts is no longer restricted as **BI capabilities** are spreading to virtually all parts of organizations as top management is striving to put critical data into the hands of business users who need it to do their jobs. The spread of BI capabilities and the power of data analysis into the hands of everyday workers brings up the question of whether or not the benefits will outweigh the risks of misuse of the data. The outcome will be questionable unless steps are taken to deploy adequate security tools and processes to protect the integrity and privacy of the BI data; BI training needs to be mandatory for end users, not just training in how to use a BI tool, but why to use the tool in the first place. Managers should ensure that only those workers who stand to benefit from the information gained be allowed to use it and that only BI vendor products be used that nonstatisticians are able to benefit from their use (Betts 2004).

BEYOND WISDOM

THE CONTINUED INCIDENTS of school violence are only one of the many indicators that our **educational system needs redirection**. This is a single need of the many needs for the organization, funding, and operation of the knowledge development agency (KDA). A much greater need is the elimination of the segregation problems that, after fifty years, since *Brown v. Board of Education*, still troubles the education industry. By 2004 there were still 11 states awaiting federal declarations that their college systems are fully integrated. We have condoned hazing of freshmen when they enter high school, fraternity pledges, and probably the most severe of all, the incoming students at our military schools along with special military units that have their own code of requirements. No matter how bad things may become, these problems turn on the lights as to where action must be taken and the problems solved sometimes for repeated times. We need to reflect on our treatment of each other and see what needs to be done to correct the results of apparent mistakes in our educational system as it exists today. The KDA has more work that needs to be accomplished than previously envisioned in this report.

Under today's circumstances, something needs to be done to upgrade our educational system. Many teachers recognize that they are entrusted with nurturing the minds, hearts, and souls of the students they teach. Few have had little if any training except the indoctrination of the First Amendment's separation of church and state. Seldom is this requirement explained in detail except to leave the meaning as stated by **Professor Linda Lantieri** that she "was forbidden to discuss with my students a vital source of purpose and meaning in my own life." She had been raised in a faith-based home, and "my spiritual experience was and is still a central and defining aspect of my life. It was a part of me, I concluded, that was not welcome in my classroom and (in) my teaching. And so my very rewarding life as a teacher was also a divided one—a life of not being able, to paraphrase the words of Parker Palmer, to live on the outside the truth I knew on the inside" (Lantieri 2001).

Professor Lantieri believed that it was possible for schools to nurture the hearts and spirits of the students in ways that do not violate the beliefs of families or the constitutional principle of the separation of church and state. She also believed that teaching the whole child can include welcoming the wisdom of a child's soul into the classrooms. After all, as she concluded, "the original intent of the First Amendment was to protect our nation from the establishment of any specific religion or dogma while giving all citizens the right to freely express their own beliefs. It certainly was never meant to suffocate such an important part of life as our spiritual experience." With full realization that bringing forth a book about welcoming the spiritual dimension into public schools was risky, she also realized that she was well aware of how far she was deviating from the status quo. What she was attempting in her book, *Schools with Spirit*, was to build a bridge between the inner life of mind and spirit and the outer world of secular education with the help of numerous contributors with a variety of personal experiences, all pointing toward the same goal (Lantieri 2001; Hebel 2004).

Since Lantieri's book was published in 2001, corporate scandals have prompted many business schools to create courses on business ethics, which sometimes touch on religion and morals. MBA students learn plenty about quantitative values; now more students are getting lessons in spiritual values, as well. More schools are offering courses dealing with spirituality and personal fulfillment in the workplace. What they want to teach students is the importance of remaining true to their convictions—whether rooted in organized religion or personal morality—amid the conflicting demands and temptations they will likely confront during their careers. For example, at the Instituto de Empresa business school in Madrid, students' religious beliefs come into play in ethics class when they discuss the marketing of RU-486, the so-called abortion pill. However, the courses that deal specifically with spirituality and values get much more personal. They aim to increase self-awareness and the desire for more spiritually rewarding jobs. Dr. Srikumar Rao, who teaches "Creativity and Personal Mastery" at Columbia University Business School says, "work hours are so grueling these days that if you don't love what you do, you are in hell" (Alsop 2005).

As I was preparing to write the section of this report on wisdom, I became convinced that one of my recommendations would be that all college students should be required to take one **course in philosophy**. Little did I realize at the time that one of the contributors to the book *Schools with Spirit* was Jacob Needleman, a professor of philosophy at San Francisco State University, who had taught a course in philosophy to students at San Francisco University High School (Needleman 2001).

RECOMMENDATIONS

I REPEAT MY 1994 recommendation that the Departments of Education and Labor be merged into a new **department of knowledge development.** The major objective of the knowledge development concept is to prepare individuals to become self-sufficient and able to compete in a very competitive environment. We can no longer rely on lifetime employment with an organization. Students must equip themselves with knowledge that will be in demand by many different organizations and then use the knowledge in developing wisdom as they gain experience. Although the concept must provide opportunity to learn how to work in groups and as teams, it is individual leadership where the greatest rewards will be found in the development of personal knowledge **(PKD)**. This new department would put emphasis on the development of knowledge rather than having a split effort of training a major portion of our workforce by the Department of Labor while the other half are educated by the Department of Education. To meet the objectives, the knowledge development concept will redirect the national education and training efforts toward meeting the needs of all organizations across the land.

In 1995, in **England**, the Departments of Education and Employment were merged. These departments are similar to our Departments of Education and Labor. Since the merger, all available reports indicate that it has been a success. The only change seems to be in the name. It is now called the **Department of Education and Skills** (Clark 2003).

Although there appears to be many more advantages than disadvantages resulting from the proposed merger of the Departments of Education and Labor, this is not a recommendation that should be undertaken by the **knowledge development agency (KDA)** proposed in the following paragraph. **Congress** needs to evaluate this proposal and implement the recommendation when found to be desirable.

Preparing for the redirection of the national education and training efforts is a major national effort, like building the atomic bomb or landing a man on the moon. These efforts required the Manhattan Project and the National

Aeronautics and Space Administration (NASA). In order to meet this need, we must organize and fund a **knowledge development agency** (**KDA**), similar to these two national efforts. Although I first made this recommendation over a decade ago, in 1994, but now we have an additional need in the **No Child Left Behind Act** that cleared Congress in a bipartisan landslide in 2001. It seems unfortunate that this act should become a debatable issue in such a short time. Therefore, it is a case of **rescue** on our part to correct its flaws and see to it that all the good points acknowledged in the beginning are implemented and that the necessary corrections in the law are made.

The historic goals of the **No Child Left Behind Act,** accepted and supported by business and civil rights groups alike, were to give every child in America a "highly qualified teacher" by 2006, and to ensure that all students achieve "proficiency" in core subjects by 2014. According to a January 2004 study, only twenty states had the required tests in place, and others, like Virginia, have voted to ask Congress for a waiver from the law and, in the case of Virginia, the state branded it as being the "most sweeping intrusion into local control of education in the history of the U.S." Some individuals who have been supportive of the law have been overcome by the negative attitudes and even admit that the time frame for implementation is unrealistic instead of finding a way to make it work (Symonds 2004).

It is disgusting to see the need for improved education within this country become a political football being kicked around oblivious of what is needed to keep the United States a leader in global competition. **A national leader** is needed to head the **KDA** with enough internal fortitude to bring about taxpayer recognition and support for the evaluation and reorganization of the educational system for the entire country. The end of WWII G.I. Bill (Servicemen's Readjustment Act) and President Kennedy's "put a man on the moon" are examples of the effort needed to bring about the necessary changes.

I am not the only one to recognize this need for the evaluation and reorganization of our educational system. In 1993, **Diane Ravitch** pointed out the "need for a stable, long-range program of research and development to guide the investment of hundreds of billions of dollars each year in education" (Ravitch 1993). For several years, **Nicholas Maxwell** has stated that "we need a revolution in the aims and methods of academic inquiry, so that the basic aim becomes to promote wisdom by rational means, instead of just to acquire knowledge" (Maxwell 2004). **Vartan Gregorian**, the president of Carnegie Corporation of New York and a former president of Brown University and the New York Public Library, stated, "clearly we have to re-evaluate our entire system of education for what it is: an 18-year learning continuum that prepares citizens for a life of learning. We must rid it of unnecessary and wasteful duplication, and create coherence and integrity in our curricula" (Gregorian 2004).

The **Educause 2004 conference** attracted more than seven thousand attendees from forty-seven different countries. The conference notebook headline in the October 29, 2004, *The Chronicle of Higher Education* read: "Technology Threatens Colleges with Extinction, Ex-President Warns." The president emeritus was James I. Duderstadt of the University of Michigan at Ann Arbor who opened the conference with unsettling predictions that the future of colleges and universities was more than uncertain in the digital age—it might be downright threatened. He quoted Guru Peter Ducker who predicted that campuses will be relics in thirty years. He also cited Frank H. T. Rhodes, president emeritus of Cornell University, saying that colleges in the digital age are like dinosaurs looking up at the incoming comet. Dr. Duderstadt also pointed out how technology has drastically changed the classroom and how faculty members have not kept up in becoming more of a guide or coach while students have gone from being passive learners to active learners and now synthesizers of knowledge (Carlson 2004b).

My recommendation for the creation of the **Knowledge Development Agency (KDA}** is for the organization of a national effort to undertake the much needed evaluation and redirection of our national education system. When this is accomplished, as a nation, we will be the leader in a global effort to lead the world in education.

Once Congress recognizes the need for an evaluation and reorganization of our national education system, appoints a bipartisan group to study the merger of the Departments of Labor and Education, and provides funding and approval of the individual to head the knowledge development agency (KDA), its work should begin. It is recognized that obtaining bipartisan congressional approval of such a large project is a monumental task; however, from all indications, the education industry needs evaluation and reorganization for the benefit of the nation as a whole. There are four major objectives for KDA action:

1. One KDA objective is to implement the concept of common standards in all grades K-12 so that students may transfer from one state to another without penalty, and then gain acceptance and support of all educational accrediting agencies for the implementation of the common standards concept in all college and university subjects and disciplines to the bachelor degree level. To some this sounds like an impossible task; however, the KDA can gain much experience by taking advantage of the *National Science Education Standards* published in 1995, and in particular Chapter 2. *Principles and Definitions*, which sets the foundation for the vision of science education reform (Standards n.d.). Much can be learned from the development of these standards and The *National Science Teaching Standards* (Standards n.d.).

2. Another KDA objective is to organize knowledge development so that the end product becomes each individual student's personal knowledge development system (PKD). This PKD will need to build on the present PKM concept; however, it changes the management of knowledge to knowledge development. PKD systems are not stand-alone systems, but systems that in each instance have network and support systems provided by the organization until graduation (Firestone 2004). At graduation, the high school, college, or university must guide each graduate in finding the necessary support needed for the continuous update of his or her PKD system during the years to come.

3. The KDA should make full use of the IES (Institute of Educational Science) of the Department of Education with the regional educational network and its ten regional educational laboratories to perform the research necessary for the recommendations that follow.

4. The KDA group must recognize that technology will be the leader in whatever direction the future of computing will take. The increasing capabilities of PDAs, smart phones, or whatever personal computing devices are developed along with increased broadband utilization, the U.S., as the leading country will inherit changes in the use of computing power in ways that are impossible to comprehend (Charlie Rose 2004).

Much work has been accomplished in developing standards for both grades and subjects. Until a common set of standards are accepted by all states, students will continue to be penalized on every move from one state to another. A national acceptance of common standards is a major effort; however, its accomplishment will make our national education system a true global leader. The implementation of the common standards for college students will do much to eliminate the fundamental problem, pointed out by President Gregorian, and referenced in the introduction, "that the present disjointed curriculum is the fragmentation of knowledge itself" (Gregorian 2004).

The end-product objective, the development of each individual student's **personal knowledge development system,** is a major effort just to gain acceptance of the concept of using PKD throughout the nation's educational system. The KDA group must determine when the students should begin the organization and operation of their PKD systems; the software recommended for student use; the support services each school, college, or university should provide; and the guidance necessary for each student's personal development of his or her own PKD. The KDA group and its research and development efforts can gain much help and guidance from the many projects under way in the personal knowledge management (PKM) area. One individual in particular, **Steve Barth,** "My Personal KM" and "The PKM Manifesto" are but two examples of his contributions. He is known internationally for his efforts

(Barth 2004). Another is Jason Frand, who describes the pioneering efforts in the development of personal knowledge management for MBA students attending the Anderson School at UCLA (Frand 2002).

The constant increasing capabilities of PDAs (personal digital assistants) and smart phones makes it hard to keep up with their latest developments; however, these small handheld computers are ideal for individual's use in the development of his or her own PKD system. This is a case where our national technology development provides for our continued national leadership. A recent Bush administration report notes that the number of Americans using broadband Internet connections doubled between 2001 and 2003; but the country as a whole still lags far behind many other nations, including South Korea, Taiwan, and Canada. The report points out the widening gap between digital haves and have-nots. Forty percent of urban area households have broadband connections compared to only 25 percent of the rural households. As a nation we are not keeping up with our competitors; we are not keeping up with countries we do not consider competitors. In view of the significant promise of PDA technology, President Bush has set out a bold vision for broadband in America, establishing a national goal for "universal, affordable access for broadband technology by the year 2007" (Cooper and Gallagher 2004).

An example of the actual use of a PDA, the handheld computer with its larger size, larger liquid crystal display using an LCD and miniature keyboard being used by a medical officer who works in family practice and also teaches in the local Kansas Medical School. To the doctor, it is like carrying a part of her office around with her. In addition to addresses, telephone numbers, e-mail addresses, schedules, class notes, references for class teaching, and several reference books on medications, geriatrics, and other references she needs, and these are only examples of what the PDA can be used for. This is an example of the type of hardware, and only one of the two major categories of PDAs now available. The second type is the palm-size computer that is smaller and uses a different type of data entry. These PDAs are typical of the hardware the PKD (personal knowledge development) user can begin with. As more and more circuitry become available on the microchip, these hardware items have sufficient capability to house all the knowledge any individual will want to keep and add to as the unit is continued in use, year after year.

The next question now is, "Should I keep a separate PDA, or buy a **smart phone** that combines the two?" In support of the smart phone, why carry two gadgets when one will do the work of both? An example of a smart phone now on the market is **palmOne Inc.**'s **Treo 600** which combines both (Wingfield 2004). However, a most important wireless development is the gradual rollout by Verizon Wireless, a technology called EV-DO that provides what is called "broadband access," an Internet access over the air from anywhere in the cities where it has been deployed (Mossberg 2004b).

Time will tell the best choice of equipment for use by individuals as they progress in the use of personal knowledge development (PKD) systems. At present, it appears that there will be adequate equipment to meet the needs.

There are many additional accomplishments that must be developed and implemented before the innovation of knowledge development. Some of these require substantial research and development prior to implementation. This is where our nation has a major advantage in that the research resources have been in operation since the **Education Sciences Reform Act of 2002** and the implementation of the IES and the research laboratories referenced above. Others require congressional approval as in the combination of the two departments, Departments of Education and Labor. The research people may find other cases where congressional approval must be obtained. To the casual reader and taxpayer, many of the following recommendations will appear to be beyond accomplishment; however, solutions must be found where problems exist, that is why the evaluation and reorganization of the national educational system is such a major national effort.

Some of the following recommendations can be carried out simultaneously with others. The order in which they are listed should not be accepted as a directive but as a suggestion to ensure inclusion of many items that could be overlooked. There are items that are not included that should be, and perhaps, some that should be dropped from the effort; however, there must be a beginning if the end is to be accomplished.

In my original 1994 knowledge development report, I pointed out that many dedicated professionals in academic institutions and cooperative organizations had developed outstanding administrative computer applications for the support of common student information systems, and that there should be a system for sharing these programs with other academic institutions. This is the beginning of one of the major objectives of the KDA group, the **development and distribution of common software** for use throughout the educational system. One example of what is to be done originated in the Kuali Project, sponsored by Indiana University and the University of Hawaii, in making financial-management software available for free in an **open source** environment to all Carnegie Class institutions. The Kuali Project Web site *http://www.kuali.org/* provides a listing of the functional elements. The design is an enhancement of the proven functionality of the Indiana University's financial information system. A critical element of the system is the XML-based EDEN© workflow for routing and approval of financial transactions. Extensive data warehousing and decision support tools will be an integral part of the system. The Kuali Project software will be modular architecture so institutions can implement only those functional elements that meet their needs (Kuali Project 2004). *The Chronicle of Higher Education* provides more details and includes comments that question the project and points out that it would be difficult to pull off, especially with so few partners, and alludes to the advantages of commercial software (Young 2004a). A later report in the information technology section B, of *The Chronicle of Higher Education* September 24, 2004, states "hundreds of colleges are betting millions of dollars they can build better software than companies can. Each has joined one or more of the many open source software projects that have emerged in recent years." The article includes a sampling, including Kuali, of eighteen open source projects in higher education (Young 2004b). According to the ACM *TechNews,* Microsoft Research India in Bangalore, "is developing new technology that will make it easier for software developers and systems integrators to add new features or modify functionality in enterprise business applications. The effort, called Rigorous Software Engineering project internally, seeks to define a system at a higher level of abstraction and generate code from it, which would allow modifications to business requirements of applications to be done at a higher level so that code does not have to be directly modified." In addition, the project also seeks to develop tools that will offer a look into systems and how they operate at abstract levels, and improve documentation of design rules and thought processes in their development (Ribeiro 2005). The KDA group should take advantage of the work being done. It is rewarding to me to see the developments taking place after my recommendation of over a decade ago.

- IBM recently donated $5 million to start a college training program in Kansas teaching open source software. The program is expected to launch during the fall of 2005 or early 2006. It is a two year program with students emerging with a certificate or going on to earn an associate's degree (Voohis 2005).

- The **software** developed for school applications and use should be made available for classroom teaching in the management information systems area. The computer science faculties and the business school faculties need to work together in using these applications in the classrooms. There are many considerations that the KDA group must be aware of during the development of this software. The following items need consideration and probably others that are not included:

- The year 2004 has been predicted as the year of the **analysis engine.** Instead of another search engine, what is needed is an analysis engine that can discern a document's meaning and then provide insight into what the search results mean in aggregate. This is what IBM is attempting to deliver in the field of machine understanding, called **Web Fountain,** an analysis engine. The KDA group should profit from IBM's work in this area (Cass 2004).

■ In the development of school applications software, the KDA group needs to be aware of the developments in **business intelligence (BI)** and how many organizations are finding it beneficial to encourage employees as well as top executives to share these capabilities often through the use of **executive dashboards,** originally called executive information systems. A dashboard is really an intranet for a select group of users. Many companies are finding it best to let employees make immediate decisions in response to opportunities rather than wait for some executive to make the decision later. There are risks in letting the power of data analysis into the hands of everyday workers who may not be qualified to use the data correctly (Kirkland 2004).

■ **Natural language processing (NLP)** and **end user development (EUD)** need the support of the KDA research and development efforts. Although quite different in objectives, these two areas have a lot in common other than the use of 4GLs in the early days of their existence. Both have the same problem of communicating with computers using a simple language users can understand and a language that can be understood by the computer. It appears that both areas are supporting extensive research in their areas and that progress is slow, but much is being accomplished. The KDA group must try to determine whether or not what is being developed in one area can be helpful in the other. It appears that promising efforts are being made in the EUD area based on a special section set of ten articles in the September 2004 issue of *Communications of the ACM* (Sutcliffe and Mehandjiev 2004). In Germany, there is a natural language software registry (NLSR), a concise summary of the capabilities and sources of a large amount of natural language processing software available to the NLP community (NLSR 2004).

■ Most colleges and universities have **data warehousing** problems that are growing daily. The use of **data mining** is gaining in recognition and use; however, it is not yet a separate discipline, but a status that should be encouraged by the KDA group. Rather than using traditional database queries, data mining proceeds by classifying and clustering data, often from a variety of different and even mutually incompatible databases, and then looking for associations. Data mining techniques enable programmers to collate and extract meaningful data from the warehouses by means of a technique called **drill down.** The data-mining software enables data warehouse users to see as much detail of summarization as they need to support their decision making normally through the use of decision support systems. The KDA should make use of the developments available in this area (Data Warehousing/Mining 2003).

- Another area the KDA should be aware of and make use of the software technology that enables analysts, managers, and executives to gain insight into data through fast, consistent, interactive access to a wide variety of possible views of information that have been transformed from raw data to reflect the real dimensionality of the enterprise as understood by the user. This is **OLAP (online analytical processing)** previously referenced in more detail in this document (OLAP 2003).

- A number of companies, such as Cisco and Oracle, have developed and use some excellent **educational software systems** for educating users in how to use their products. The KDA group needs to become aware of these and similar developments and incorporate them into software packages for instruction wherever applicable. Other examples are **Ed Compass**, from SMART Technologies Inc., one of the online communities that offer valuable resources and services for the education industry. This includes the integration of **SMART Board**, an interactive whiteboard, into teaching practices, and the **SMART interactive notebook** software (Fletcher 2004).

- **Blackboard Inc.** was founded in 1997 to help schools, districts, and education service agencies transform the Internet into a powerful environment for education. Initially, Blackboard was committed to enhancing teaching and learning in K-12 institutions and to helping schools deliver exceptional student outcomes. It soon expanded into higher education with a cross-campus learning environment that students, instructors, and other community members quickly acclimated to. It was flexible enough to support any approach to teaching, learning, research, and collaboration. Blackboard then supported corporations and government agencies as part of their blended and online learning strategies to improve the outcomes of their training and certification programs (Bb 2004).

- **Maplesoft** has had a legendary suite of products for over twenty-five years offering fundamental and critical technology to assist teaching and research in technical fields of mathematics, science, and engineering. Maple is a popular teaching tool for instructors with classes in high school mathematics. The software allows teachers to illustrate mathematical concepts, visualize problems, and illuminate theory. The software includes a set of built-in precalculus, calculus I, and linear algebra tutors designed to assist students and instructors with their educational demands. It also automates the time-consuming elements of assessment while increasing the comprehension levels in mathematics-dependent courses. These and other capabilities are also available for use in higher education and in any environment requiring mathematical and similar professional skills (Maplesoft 2004).

- Most organizations have found software useful in their management of explicit knowledge; however, their management of tacit knowledge, in most cases, they can use all the help available. Tacit knowledge, as we all know, is that knowledge in people's heads and may not be fully formed. There are hundreds of tacit knowledge software packages on the market. The word "tacit" can be confusing with some packages designed for optimization of existing applications such as performance bottlenecks. Others are designed for use in the review of source code in the context of the system on which it resides. To be more specific, the Brain Technologies Corporation's **BrainEKP** has been well recognized for its usability (BrainEKP 2003). Another is a British tacit knowledge management system called **MintMCI (managing collective intelligence).** It provides an intranet and extranet collaboration and tacit knowledge management system (Mint 2003). Tacit Knowledge Systems Inc. in Palo Alto, California, takes great pride in how one of its customers, Eastman Kodak Company, has made use of its **Tacit Knowledge Mail** software (Tacit K 2002). The KDA group will find many more software packages to draw on.

- **Teachers as coaches** are often a necessary evil where high school subjects must be taught—a teacher chosen who does not have the educational background necessary in the subject. It is in this type of situation where the teacher assumes the role of coach or mentor. The teacher would have had the opportunity to take courses and become educated in the subject prior to entering the classroom and begin teaching a subject. This is not always possible, for example, in teaching some computer programming courses, the language is no longer used in the industry setting thus requiring a change in the language to be taught is made without sufficient time for the teacher to prepare to teach the language. When this happens, the teacher learns in real time thus changing their role from being the "expert" and becomes a coach and mentor in keeping ahead of the class in their work with the new language. At the college and university level, similar situations exist when the textbook does not cover the latest development in the course or the class has found a new area that should be included. This coach or mentor relationship between students and the teacher or instructor establishes an ideal knowledge development situation.

- It is this coach-student relationship that provides the knowledge development situation that is most ideal for learning. Granted, this situation is not always possible for various reasons; some students prefer to learn on their own in their own environment without a close

74

relationship with anyone; others are reluctant to become involved with group learning, yet as individuals will find other students who have similar dispositions and enter into a close personal relationship with them as they really learn together by testing each other on new subject matter to see who is superior in understanding the material at hand. Teachers must be able to identify students by their individual styles of learning, such as a visual learner, audio learner, hands-on learner, perhaps one who learns best in a group environment, etc. This is a major undertaking each teacher faces in a classroom of twenty-five or so students and multiplied by four or five, depending on the number of classes the teacher is required to teach.

All members of the KDA group should be required to read the section entitled "**Beyond Wisdom**" as a part of their introduction to the work they will be doing in the development of software and working on the other parts of the foundation for the innovation of knowledge development. The main reason for this requirement is for all to understand and appreciate the work of Professor Linda Lantieri, documented in her book *Schools with Spirit*. She believed that something is needed to be done to upgrade our educational system. She felt that many teachers recognized that they are entrusted with nurturing the minds, hearts, and souls of the students they teach. Few teachers have had any training except the indoctrination of the First Amendment's separation of church and state (Lantieri 2001). The KDA group should also keep in mind the work being accomplished by many business schools where courses in business ethics are included. MBA students have been learning plenty about quantitative values; now they are getting lessons in spiritual values as well (Alsop 2005).

An organization's culture is possibly the most important resource used for the development of knowledge. Louis V. Gerstner Jr. as IBM CEO made the major shift in culture and in so doing did far more than the culture change by helping the flow of knowledge. In the case of Buckman Labs, it was the culture of the organization that provided the outstanding environment for knowledge management and, in particular, the sharing of knowledge. The most common description of organizational culture is that culture is really the personality of the organization. A major problem at IBM was that the organizational culture had to be changed before the company could be changed from a product-based business to that of a service-based business. When it comes to sharing knowledge, the culture of the organization dominates the reactions of the employees to either be willing to share their knowledge with others or not to share. The KDA group must keep in mind the importance of organizational culture and its presence in any organization under study. This includes the need to understand the differences in organizational cultures, just as there are differences in types of organizations (Gerstner 2002).

- A **national standard curriculum** for computer instruction for grades K-12 is needed. As an example, many students enter high school without knowledge of the keyboard, and as a result, typing classes are mandatory in high schools. The **Association for Computing Machinery (ACM)** has been continuing the development of a recommended **K-12 computer science curriculum.** The draft overview report for computing curricula 2004 and information systems' (IS) role in it is now available for comment and located on the ACM Web site, http://www.acm.org. The report also includes a guide to undergraduate degrees in computing, including computer engineering, computer science, information systems, information technology, and software engineering. These programs are under development by a joint task force for computing curricula 2004, a cooperative project of the Association for Computing Machinery (ACM), the Association for Information Systems (AIS), and The Computer Society (IEEE-CS) (Gorgone 2004). The KDA group needs to take advantage of the work under development while establishing a new national standard curriculum. The KDA group must look at other disciplines that are doing similar development and have, or need to have, curriculums for their subjects. This is another example where the KDA group can provide the leadership needed to help all subject areas.

- **As a nation**, we must recognize the excessive increases in data accumulating from day to day. We must also improve our methods of selecting those data to be used as information, the information to be used as knowledge, and in developing wisdom. This is a major undertaking, a large portion of the effort envisioned to be undertaken by the **KDA.** It begins with the need to support the implementation of **information life-cycle management (ILM)** to manage data from the cradle to the grave. ILM has a goal of putting certain types of data on appropriate storage devices and media depending on how long the data must be kept or how soon the data will have to be retrieved. This area needs constant improvement with the development of new techniques for the storage of data in particular where there are additional data storage requirements such as those resulting from meeting the requirements of **HIPAA** and **Sarbox** explained in the chapter on "Data."

- The **KDA effort** needs to complete the transition from **information resource management (IRM)** to that of **chief information officer,** making the **CIO concept** used far and wide across the country and at all levels where it may apply. The CIO Council should assume a role of national leadership rather than the present apparently limited role for governmental agencies. All efforts need to be pointed toward obtaining intellectual input in the way of guidance for the improvement of information management across the nation from the **research board,** owned by Gartner Inc. and based in New York City.

- **The KDA group** must continue to recognize that **libraries** have long been remembered as the information centers of cities, organizations, schools, colleges, and universities. It is now time to make libraries the centers for knowledge development. Libraries need to change their mission from that of providing information to that of providing information and knowledge wherever possible, and in guiding individuals in their use of **personal knowledge development (PKD)** systems. This includes making use of the latest in PDA or smart phone hardware. Additional missions are in helping individuals develop networking and communications for use in building, maintaining, and expanding their PKDs year after year, while still in school, and after graduation.

- The KDA group must also continue to be aware of the possible changes that are likely to take place in the realignment of library organizations and usage. The arrival of the digital age has given birth to entirely new formats of scholarly communications, like online databases, e-journals, e-books that today are only the seeds of what will come. Drastic changes are inevitable in the ways libraries and scholarly publishers operate, and in the way reference material is operated in the near future (Dillon 2004).

- A more recent example of the likely changes in library operation, although in the same month (December 2004) after the Dennis Dillon article, is Google adding major libraries to its database. An agreement was announced December 14, 2004 between Google and some of the leading research libraries and Oxford University to begin converting their holdings into digital files that would be freely searchable over the Web. It is true that this may be only a step on a long road toward the long-predicted global virtual library; but the collaboration of Google and research institutions that also include Harvard, the University of Michigan, Stanford, and the New York Public Library is a major stride in an ambitious Internet effort by various parties. The goal is to expand the Web beyond its current valuable, if eclectic, body of material and create a digital card catalog and searchable library for the world's books, scholarly papers, and special collections. Google is able to begin funding for the project due to the cash it accumulated from the IPO last summer. Google's agreements with the various libraries are slightly different—eight million books in Stanford's collection, seven million at

Michigan; the Harvard project will initially be limited to only about forty thousand volumes, and the Bodleian Library at Oxford will be limited to an unspecified number of books published before 1900. Google and Amazon, along with a dozen major publishing companies, have as a primary target for the online text-search efforts allowing users to search the text of copyrighted books online and read excerpts (Markoff and Wyatt 2004).

Since Google announced that it would work with five of the world's largest libraries in an effort to scan millions of books and make the full texts part of its popular search index, *The Chronicle of Higher Education* initiated a project to obtain comments from five key players on Google's project and its meaning. These are summarized and published in the Information Technology section of the June 3, 2005 issue of *The Chronicle of Higher Education* and include comments from favorable to questionable (Young 2005). In addition, this section includes the announcement by Jean-Noel Jeanneney, president of the National Library of France in the form of a call to arms to European librarians urging them to mount a large-scale digital library of their own. By May, 2005, 23 national libraries in the European Union announced their support for the European digital-library project (Labi 2005).

Students must be recognized as the education industry's **most valuable resource**. The Elementary and Secondary Act of 1965 (ESEA) and the National Defense Education Act of 1958 were the only major changes in shaping the role of education policy since the Morel Act at the time of the Civil War. It was thought that Title I of the ESEA would provide for the education of African-American students and those known as "educationally deprived." Unfortunately, at the time there was no way of measuring the success or failure of the Act. Since 1965, providing equal opportunities has no longer been sufficient. The goal was changed to provide equal or nearly equal outcomes for all. Public schools now have the responsibility to educate all children under the mandates of the No Child Left Behind legislation, the latest reauthorization of ESEA. The setting of minimum standards and holding all students accountable for reaching that low level, a ceiling has been placed on both expectations and outcomes. Some believe that gifted programs are not necessary as long as the resources are available to the gifted students; on the other hand, many believe (and this author for one) that gifted programs are necessary (Lagemann 2005).

K-12 schools as centers of their communities have been recommended since my original 1994 report. Communities need a center for their activities, a meeting place, and a recognized gathering point within their community. Students and their parents who participate in **home-**

schooling should be included in the use of these schools that are the centers of their communities. The school is the most convenient, most accessible, and in most cases the most useful facility to serve this needed resource. As community centers, the schools will become useful as knowledge development centers for all members of the community. In order to provide this resource on a continuing basis, the schools need to be operated **full-time, year-round**. These recommendations were contained in my original 1994 report and are continued. The National Association for Year-Round Education's report for 2003 identified more than 2.3 million students attending year-round schools in forty-six states (YRE 2003). It is most unfortunate that as a nation we are still bound by the old agricultural need to let students out in the early summer to help put in the crops and tend them.

As this is being written, **outsourcing** is still gathering momentum. Referenced in the information section, out of **101 IT executives surveyed**, 26 had offshore call centers, and 86 percent said they had offshore computer application developments. India's market share keeps growing as does that of other countries. Neighbors in Canada and Mexico are now handling highly complex projects, and new members of the European Union are an enticing resource for Western European companies and European-based U.S. businesses (Datz 2004).

Something that should not be overlooked in outsourcing is the **transfer of knowledge** to an offshore vendor that can include everything from programming expertise to what users expect from a system. This can make or break an outsourced project. CIOs who are involved with outsourcing must understand the full extent of knowledge that must be transferred and that knowledge that must not be transferred (Overby 2004).

Because **expert systems** are a quick, understandable way of moving tacit knowledge into explicit knowledge, more emphasis is needed to expand the development and use of expert systems. These expert systems are knowledge-based systems in the field of artificial intelligence. Conventional programming languages such as C, C++, or Java are designed and optimized for the procedural manipulation of data, such as numbers and arrays. Humans often solve complex problems using very abstract, symbolic approaches which are not well suited for implementation in conventional programming languages. Although abstract information can be modeled in these languages, considerable programming effort is required to transform the information to a format usable with procedural programming paradigms. Research in the area of artificial intelligence has been the development of techniques which allow the modeling of information at higher levels of abstraction. These techniques are embodied in languages or tools which allow programs to be built that closely resemble human logic in their implementation and are therefore easier to develop and maintain (Railey 2004). The KDA effort to expand the development and use of expert systems must take into consideration the latest developments produced by the research in artificial intelligence. Every effort should be made to expand the use of the expert system software called **CLIPS (C language integrated production system)** now maintained independently as public domain software (CLIPS FAQ 2004). The same support needs to be given other expert systems useful in other areas. In particular, support is needed where expert systems are developed for special fields such as in the field of medicine. The KDA effort must become aware of the research and developments that are in progress and support these efforts.

Many organizations and government agencies have developed their own successful **knowledge management systems**. Whenever possible, these should be recognized and applauded. Organizations, like Buckman Laboratories, which does not use the knowledge management concept nor have a CKO, yet has outstanding methods of organizing, maintaining, increasing, and making the organization's knowledge available. These organizations should be encouraged to continue to improve their own systems and provide ideas helpful to others.

Students must take responsibility for developing wisdom. It is no longer a class project but an individual undertaking. Guidance can be provided in class to encourage wisdom development, but it is the individual that recognizes the need and creates the desire to develop wisdom. As wisdom is developed in one discipline or a subject area within a discipline, the student needs to be encouraged to apply transference to another subject or discipline. Much of the wisdom development can be accomplished while still in school through the study and understanding of individuals who had experiences that have demonstrated wisdom development. For example, those individuals who have made mistakes but have been able to correct the mistakes profited from the experience. In many cases, the development of wisdom will come about after course completion and graduation.

The KDA group should support Professor Peter Denning in his efforts to have **information technology** recognized **as a profession**. After all, it is technology that is leading and will continue to lead the way in developing our computer-supported future in research, business, government, and education. As a nation, we have been most fortunate in our ability to maintain the leadership in technology development and technology applications. Now that we are competing on a global playing field, it is all the more important that we maintain this leadership in the future. The recognition of technology was given full credit for whatever happens in the future of computing by a most distinguished group of CEOs who met November 17, 2004, in the Google offices in Mountain View, California. Eric Schmidt, the CEO of Google Inc., acted as host for the following who were in attendance: John Chambers, CEO of Cisco Inc.; Paul Otillini, CEO of Intel Inc.; and Terry Semel, CEO of Yahoo! Inc. The group was presented by Charlie Rose, the award-winning journalist, on his TV program. The corporate leaders stressed the need for **convergence**, the act of moving toward union or uniformity in all their undertakings with special emphasis on technology, the expanding capabilities of personal digital assistants (PDAs) and smart phones plus the need for increased use of broadband support across the land (Charlie Rose 2004).The recommended use of personal knowledge development (PKD) in this report appears to be in agreement with the thinking of these men who made up the panel.

- During the research for the section on wisdom, I became exposed to the study of philosophy to a much greater extent than ever before. As a result, I am convinced that all college students should be required to take **one course in philosophy.**

- The KDA group should organize and develop a required course suitable in high school or college to educate students in **individual finance** so that they will not become victims of credit card abuse to the extent that they charge items until they can only afford to pay interest.

- The contributions by the **text retrieval conferences (TREC)** since they were started in 1992 to support research within the information retrieval community should be recognized and supported by the KDA group (TREC 2004).

- **"Making Them Pay"** describes how online businesses are learning how to make money charging for information they can make available for a fee (Totty 2004). This is an area that the KDA group needs to watch and see how it will impact information retrieval.

- **Spyware or adware,** are the newest, most virulent, and least understood, malicious software programs, different from viruses, spam, or hacker attacks. The antiviruses, antispam, or firewall programs you may already use do little or nothing to fight spyware because these programs were written to solve other problems. As their names imply, these programs try to steal your private information, record your behavior, and transmit it to others, and turn your PC into an engine for displaying ads. They can alter your Web browser and make it use a bogus home page or search engine. In the worst case, they can steal your identity. Switching to an Apple Macintosh is the absolute best way to avoid spyware. Mossberg recommends three programs; of the three, even though it costs a little money, it's called **Spy Sweeper** from Webroot at *http://www.webroot.com* (Mossberg 2004c).

- The KDA group must determine the role **Vocational Education** needs to play in high school reform.
- The KDA group must acquire and maintain the support of **private foundations** and other philanthropic organizations in their effort to evaluate and reorganize the U.S. education system for the nation.
- The KDA group should evaluate the teacher certification systems now in use and provide a national system of K-12 teacher certification that will permit a K-12 teacher, once certified, to teach in any state in the United States.

Conclusions

THIS REPORT DOCUMENTS a method to accomplish the redirection of the national education system in this country so that we may maintain the leadership now being challenged by other nations around the globe. A major national effort, similar to building the atomic bomb or landing a man on the moon, is required. A **knowledge development agency (KDA)** has been recommended throughout this report to be funded and organized to direct the efforts that have been outlined, plus other efforts that will materialize as work is accomplished. The **most important objective of the KDA group is obtaining congressional support of the knowledge development** concept as outlined. The second most important objective of the KDA group is **to obtain union support** of the knowledge development concept, and third, to **gain national support** of national common standards for grades and subjects throughout the land. Physics 1 should not be different for students in Maine than for students in California. States must recognize that education is truly a national effort, just as they must recognize that we no longer need students to be released early in the spring to put in the crops and tend them.

My original 1994 knowledge development report pointed out the need for schools to develop and distribute common software for use throughout the education system. This is now being done in numerous projects where colleges and universities are betting that they can build better software than companies can.

The innovation of the knowledge development concept will be complete when the common standards concept has been applied in all grades, subjects, and disciplines across the country, and students have their own personal knowledge development systems in operation for use during the remainder of their lifetimes. To make this possible, elementary, middle, and high schools along with colleges and universities must accept and support the knowledge development concept for all grades, subjects, and disciplines.

Knowledge development innovation will provide this nation with the ability to demonstrate a global leadership role in education, making use of the latest improvements in information technology, with faculty technically qualified to fulfill their role as guides or coaches, with students as active learners and synthesizers of knowledge. It is impossible at this time to predict the outcomes of the information technology developments; however, our education system must remain flexible and be ready to implement whatever new developments become available.

The KDA group needs the support of Microsoft Research. This research effort focuses on long-term (10-15 years out) computer science research and vision that is not bound by product cycles. Microsoft Research effort has evolved into an organization with more than 700 researchers studying more than 55 research areas (Microsoft Research 2006).

There have been hundreds of efforts to develop solutions to the problems of our troubled public schools. So far, out of all the efforts, not one has been recognized as a solution that should be implemented throughout the land. The leading effort has been the work of Bill and Melinda Gates who have had some limited successes along with nationally recognized failures. The KDA group must recognize the extent of the problem (Greene and Symonds 2006).

Senators Pete Domenici (R-NM), Jeff Bingaman (D-NM), Lamar Alexander (R-TN), and Barbara Mikulski (D-MD) introduced three Senate Bills that collectively, made up the Protecting America's Competitive Edge (PACE) Act. The three bills are S.2197, S. 2198, and S.2199. The object of the PACE Act is to help America maintain its leading edge in mathematics, science, engineering, and technology. When enacted and funded, the PACE Act will contribute what is needed for the four areas (Press Releases 2006).

According to Senior CIO Writer Ben Worthen, who went to China in early 2006 to research **the next generation Internet** found that in research labs throughout China, engineers are busy working on China's Next Generation Internet (CNGI), planned to be unveiled during the 2008 Olympics, that will be faster, more secure, and a more mobile version than the current one. Worthen believes that the CNGI's impact will be felt for ages, and that it is the centerpiece of China's plan to steal leadership away from the United States in all things Internet and information technology (Worthen 2006).

BIBLIOGRAPHY

Agresti, William W. 2003. "Discovery Informatics." *Communications of the ACM* 46, no. 8 (August 2003): 25-28.

Alsop, Ronald. 2005. "M.B.A. Track" *Wall Street Journal* January 11, 2005, B6.

Article Central. 2004. "SPAM Growth Prompts Email Decline" Pew Internet and American Life Project. March 24, 2004. *http://www.thewhir.com/find/articlecentral/story.asp?recordid=8* (accessed March 24, 2004).

Bank, David. 2003. "Open Source Database Poses Oracle Threat." *Wall Street Journal* July 9, 2003, B1.

———. 2004. "More Old Software Is 'Open Sourced'" *Wall Street Journal* July 8, 2004, B5.

Bank, David and William Bulkeley. 2003. "In About-Face, Siebel to Deliver Software on Net." *Wall Street Journal* October 2, 2003, B1.

Barth, Steve. 2004. *http://www.global-insight.com/pkm/* (accessed November 2, 2004).

Bartlett, Bruce. 2004."The Shipping News." *Wall Street Journal* July 24, 2004, D-10.

Bb. 2004. "Explore Blackboard" <http://www.blackboard.com/k12/index.htm> (accessed December 2, 2004).

Bellinger, Gene, Durval Castro, and Anthony Mills. 2004. "Data, Information, Knowledge, and Wisdom" February 2, 2004. <http://www.systems-thinking.org/dikw.htm.> (accesed August 12, 2004).

Bender-Samuel, et. al. 2003. "The Correct Way to Sole Source, Part 2" *Outsourcing Journal,* November 2003. *http://www.outsourcing-journal.com/nov2003-everest.html* (accessed November 27, 2003).

Bettoni, Marco C. 2002. "Individual Knowledge Management with MailTrack." 13th International Workshop on Database and Expert Systems Applications (DEXA '02) Aix-en-Provence, France, 157 *http://csdl.computer.org/comp/proceedings/dexa/2002/1668/00/1* (accessed February 19, 2004).

Betts, Mitch. 2003. "Knowledge Center Storage." *Computerworld* November 17, 2003, 25.

———. 2004. "The Future of BI." *Computerworld* June 21, 2004, 37-45.

Borzo, Jeanette. 2004. "Get the Picture." *Wall Street Journal* January 12, 2004, R4.

BrainEKP. 2003. "BrainEKP Named a Trend-Setting Product of 2003 by KMWorld." *http://www.thebrain.com/company/Press/releases/released43.html* (accessed December 16, 2003).

Brannan, Linda. 2004. e-mail message to the author, November 11, 2004.

Buckman, Bob. 2003. "Common Sense: Peersonal Decision-Making—Bob Buckman" January 20, 2003. *AOK_K-Net@yahoogroups.com* (accessed January 21, 2004).

Bulkeley, William M. 2004a. "IBM Documents Give Rare Look at Offshoring." *Wall Street Journal* January 19, 2004, A1.

———. 2004b. "IBM Posts 17% Increase in Earnings." *Wall Street Journal* July 16, 2004, A3.

Carlson, Scott. 2004a."To Use that Library Computer, Please Identify Yourself." *The Chronicle of Higher Education* June 25, 2004, A39.

———. 2004b. "Technology Threatens Colleges with Extinction, Ex-President Warns." *The Chronicle of Higher Education* October 29, 2004, A34.

Cass, Stephen. 2004. "A Fountain of Knowledge 2004 will be the year of the analysis engine." *IEEE SPECTRUM http://www.spectrum.ieee.org/WEBONLY/publicfeature/jan04/0* (accessed January 27, 2004).

Census.2000. "The U.S. Census Collection." *http://www.ancestry.com/landing/product/search/census.aspx?S* (accessed November 19, 2003).

Census. 2002. "Software and Data Catalog." *http://www.tetrad.com/pub/documents/SF1.pdf* (accessed November 20, 2003).

Charlie Rose. 2004. Charlie Rose Show November 17, 2004. *http://www.charlierose.com/search/search.asp* (Accessed November 20, 2003).

Christian, Eliot. 2003. e-mail message to the author, November 16, 2003.

CIO Navy. 2003 <http://www.doncio.navy.mil/(raief455rlirncfmzillo555)/main.as> (accessed November 26, 2003).

CIO Utah. 2003. <http:www.cio.state.ut.us/> (accessed November 26, 2003).

CiteSeer. 2003. NCR Research Institute CiteSeer. *http://citeseer.nj.nec.com* (accessed January 28, 2003).

Clarke, Charles. 2003. "The Future of Higher Education." *http://www.dfes.gov.uk;highereducation;docs;white%20Pape.pdf* (accessed November 15, 2003).

Clementine. 2004. "Quickly turn data into better business results." *http://www.spss.com/clementine/?source=kdnuggets&campaign* (accessed August 23, 2004).

CLIPS FAQ. 2004."CLIPS Frequently Asked Questions." May 22, 2004. *http://www.ghg.net/clips/CLIPS-FAQ* (accessed July 30, 2004).

CLO. 2003. *http://www.clomedia.com* (accessed November 26, 2003).

Cooper, Kathleen and Michael D. Gallagher. 2004. "A Nation Online: Entering the Broadband Age." *http://www.ntia.doc.gov/reports/anol/NationOnlineBroadband04.doc* (accessed November 27, 2004).

Core Knowledge. 2004. *http://www.coreknowledge.org* (accessed July 20, 2004).

Data Warehousing/Mining. 2003. *Webster's New World Computer Dictionary.* 10th ed. 2003.

Datz, Todd. 2003. "Storage Essentials." *CIO Magazine* October 15, 2003, 105-111.

――――. 2004. "Outsourcing World Tour." *CIO Magazine* July 15, 2004, 42-48.

Davis, Stan and Jim Botkin. 1994. "The Coming of Knowledge-Based Business." *Harvard Business Review* September-October 1994, 165-174.

Delaney, Kevin J. 2004. "Google Software to Search PCs Takes Aim at Microsoft's Turf." *Wall Street Journal* October 15, 2004, b8.

DHS Organization. 2003. "DHS Organization, Leadership, Chief Privacy Officer: Nuala O'Connor Kelly." <http://www.dhs.gov/dhspublic/interappo/biography _O> (accessed November 25, 2003).

Denning, Peter. 2001. "The Profession of IT." *Communications of the ACM* February 2001. 44, no. 2, 15-19.

Dillon, Dennis. 2004. "College Libraries: The Long Goodbye." *The Chronicle of Higher Education* December 10, 2004, B5.

Durant, Will. 1961. *The Story of Philosophy.* A Touchtone Book, Simon and Schuster.

Education. 2004. "Education in Data Mining and Knowledge Discovery" *http://www.kdnuggets.com/education/index.html* (accessed August 23, 2004).

Edvinsson, Leif, et al. 2003. "KM in Europe." *Knowledge Board http://www.knowledgeboard.com/cgi-bin/item.cgi?id=120130&d* (accessed November 21, 2003).

English, Larry. 2004. "Data Quality Standardize, Validate and Improve Your Information Assets." *http://www.dataflux.com/data/dataqual.pdf* (accessed June 27, 2004).

FGDC. 2003. "The Geographic Foundation of America's Information-Based Society." *http://www.fgdc.gov/publications/nsdi_gos.html* (accessed August 23, 2004).

5GL Doctor. 2004."Doctor Self-Diagnosis Software." *http://members.ozemail.com.au/~lisadev/sftdocpu.htm* (accessed September 8, 2004).

5GL Fifth Generation. 1984-1990. *http://csepl.phy.oral.gov/ov/node14.html* (accessed July 25, 2004).

Firestone, Joe. 2004. "IPKM: Progress of All Forms of KM Depends on the Other." AOK_K-Net Digest Number 330. February 27, 2004. From Jerry Ash *jash@kwork.org. http://www.macroinnovation.com/nkm.htm* (accessed February 28, 2004).

Fleischer, Joe. 2003. "Wedding Knowledge and Content." December 2, 2003. *http://www.callcenteermagazine.com/shared/article/showArticle.J* (accessed December 22, 2003).

Fletcher, Geoffrey. 2004."New Virtual Classroom Community, Whiteboarding Competition Provide Educators With 'SMART' Resources." August 10, 2004. *http://www.thejournal.com/thefocus/deatureprintversion.cfm?ne* (accessed August 30, 2004).

FOCUS. 2004. "FOCUS Report Writer." *http://helpdesk.ysu.edu/news/vol1.1/11focus.htm* (accessed August 10, 2004).

Foundations. 2004. "Where is the Wisdom We Have Lost in Knowledge?" *http://www.foundationsmag.com/wisdom.html* (accessed April 7, 2004).

Frand, Jason. 2002. "Personal Knowledge Management: A Strategy for Controlling Information Overload." February 4, 2002, DRAFT and "Personal Knowledge Management: Who, What, Why, When, Where, How." December 1999. *http://www.anderson.ucla.edu/faculty/jason. frand/researcher* (accessed October 12, 2004).

Fuld, Leonard M. 1998. "Knowledge Profiteering." *CIO ENTERPRISE.* Section 2. June 15, 1998, 28-32.

Gerstner, Louis V. Jr. 2002. *"Who Says Elephants Can't Dance? Inside IBM's Historic Turnaround."* New York: HarperCollins, 2002, 30-41, 61, 97-109, 171-177, 255-257.

GILS. 2003. "A Powerful New Way to Find Information" *http://www.gils. net/locator.html* (accessed November 17, 2003).

Goals. 2000. "Goals 2000: Educate America Act." *http://www.ed.gov/ legislation/GOALS2000/The Act/index.html* (accessed November 10, 2004).

Goetz, Martin. 1996. "A 4GL Future?—Fourth Generation Languages for Creating Enterprise Applications-Technology Information Column." *Software Magazine.* March, 1996. *http://www.findarticles.com/p/articles/ mi_mOSMG/is_n3_v16/ai* (accessed September 4, 2004).

Gorgone, John T. 2004. "Information Systems and the Overview Report for Computing Curricula 2004." SIGCSE Bulletin *inroads* 36, no. 4, (December 2004), 15-16.

Greene, Jay, and William C. Symonds. 2006. "Bill Gates Gets Schooled" Business Week June 26, 2006, 65-70.

Gregorian, Vartan. 2004. "Colleges Must Reconstruct the Unity of Knowledge." *The Chronicle of Higher Education* June 4, 2004, B12-B14.

Grossman, Lev. 2004. "Meet Joe Blog." *Time* June 21, 2004, 63-70.

Hagland, Mark. 2003. "Doctor's Orders." *Healthcare Informatics* *http://www.healthcare-informatice.com/issues/2003/01_03/cpoe* (accessed September 10, 2004).

Hamblen, Matt. 2003. "Keeping a Safe Distance." *Computerworld* November 17, 2003, 42.

Hawthorne, David. n.d. "Conversations with Tom Stewart—Part II. Star Series" *http://www.kwork.org/Stars/stewart_part2.html* (accessed April 19, 2004).

Hebel, Sara. 2004. "Segregation's Legacy Still Troubles Campuses." *The Chronicle of Higher Education* May 14, 2004, A24-A27.

Holden, John and E. D. Hirsch Jr. (Ed.) 1996. *Books to Build on* New York: Dell Publishing a division of Bantam Doubleday Dell Publishing Group, 13-14.

Horton, Forest Woody Jr. 1979. *Information Resources Management: Concept and Cases.* Cleveland, OH: Association for Systems Management, 74.

Hsu, William H. 2003. "Laboratory for Knowledge Discovery in Databases (KDD)." *http://www.kddresearch.org/Info/* (accessed August 17, 2004).

IBM. 2003. "Business Transformation Outsourcing." *http://www-1.ibm. com/services/bcs/bto_home.html?ca=ondema* (accessed November 27, 2003).

IBM Lotus Workplace. 2003. "The human e-business on demand." *http:// www-306.ibm.com/software/swnews/swnews.nsf/n/jmae5s* (accessed November 27, 2004).

IES 2004. "The Regional Laboratory Network." *http://www.mcrel.org/rel/ network.asp* (accessed November 3, 2004).

Institute. 2003. 27 Nov. 2003. *http://www.outsourcing.com/* (accessed October 4, 2003).

Johnson, Maryfran. 2001. "Inside the CIO Brain Trust." *Computerworld* May-June 2001, 25-28. *http://www.computerworld.com/ROI.*

Kanesshige, Tom. 2003. "Counter Culture." *Portals Magazine* July 2003. *http:// www. askmecorp.com/julyportals.asp* (accessed December 3, 2003).

Kankanhalli, Atreyi, et al. 2003. "The Role of IT in Successful Knowledge Management Initiatives." *Communications of the ACM* September 2003, 46, no. 9, 69-73.

Kelly, Chris. 2001. "Oh No, Not Another O!" *CIO Magazine* January 15, 2001, 86-87.

Kirkland, Alex. 2004. "Executive Dashboards." <*http://www.boxesand*arrows.com/archives/executive_dashboards> (accessed July 23, 2004).

Kirkpatrick, David. 2004a."How Open-Source World Plans to Smack Down Microsoft, and Oracle." *Fortune* February 23, 2004, 92-100.

———. 2004b. "Inside Sam's $100 billion growth machine." *Fortune* June 14, 2004, 80-98.

KMFeature. 2000. "Your Say Part 2: Document Management vs. Knowledge Management." *http://www.kmmagazine.com/xq/asp/sid.AB1EAC7C-30AC-443* (accessed December 8, 2003).

Koch, Christopher. 2004. "The Sarbox Conspiracy" *CIO Magazine* July 1, 2004, 59-68.

Kuali Project. 2004. "The Kuali Project." *http://www.kuali.org/* (accessed July 9, 2004}.

Labi, Aisha. 2005. "A French Library Leader Urges a European Response. "From Gutenberg to Google." *The Chronicle of Higher Education* June 3, 2005, A27.

Lantieri, Linda. 2001. *Schools with Spirit*. Boston, MA: Beacon Press, xi-xvii.

Lagemann, Ellen Condiffe. 2005."A Commitment to Equity What Matters About the Elementary and Secondary Act of 1965" *Education Week* April 13, 2005 24 no. 31, 60-61.

LifeLog. 2002. "Your life at your fingertips-courtesy of the Pentagon." *http://www.usatoday,com/tech/news/techinnovations/2003-06-02* (accessed June 4, 2003).

LifeLog. 2003. "LifeLog Technical Program." *http://www.darpa.mil/ipto/programs/lifelog/* (accessed December 16, 2003).

Linux. 2003. "What is Linux?" *http://www.linux.org/info/index.html* (accessed November 29, 2003).

Loftus, Peter. 2003. "Information-Technology Firms Battle as Outsourcing Expands." *Wall Street Journal*, September 24, 2003, B13A.

Lundberg, Abbie. 2004. "The Best and Worst of Times." *CIO Magazine* October 1, 2004, 12.

Malhotra, Yogesh. 2003. "Integrating Knowledge Management Technologies in Organizational Business Processes: Getting Real Time Enterprises to Deliver Real Business Performance." Accepted for publication in the *Journal of Knowledge Management* (Emerald) Special Issue on "Knowledge Management and Technology," Q3, 2004. *http://www.kmnetwork.com/KnowledgeManagementRealTimeEnterpriseBush* (accessed December 5, 2003).

Manville, Michael. 2003. "City of Knowledge, Panama Canal Zone." *http://panamaatyourservice.com/Technology/city_knowledge_art.* (accessed December 12, 2003).

Maplesoft. 2004. "Academic." *http://www.maplesoft.com/academic/index.aspx* (accessed December 3, 2004).

Markoff, John and Edward Wyatt. 2004. "Google Is Adding Major Libraries to Its Database." *http://www.nytimes.com/2004/12/14/technology/14google. html* (accessed December 14, 2004).

Martin, James. 1985. *Fourth Generation Languages*. Prentice-Hall, 1985.

Maxwell, Nicholas. 2004. "We Need a Revolution." *http://www.nick-maxwell. demon.co.uk* (accessed October 6, 2004).

McGovern, Gerry. 2003. "Why content management software hasn't worked." *http://www.gerrymcgovern.com/nt/2003/nt_2003_03_03_cms.h* (accessed January 23, 2004).

Mearian, Lucas. 2003a. "Tape Technology Stretches Out." *Computerworld* September 1, 2003, 20.

———. 2003b. "The Data Life Cycle." *Computerworld* November 17, 2003, 38-40.

Med Exp Sys. 2004. Medical Expert Systems. *http://www.computer.privateweb. at/judith/special_field3.htm* (accessed February 6, 2004).

Meeker, Joseph W. 2003. "Wisdom and Wilderness." *http://www.cop.com/ info/wisdompg.html* (accessed January 3, 2004).

Meetings. 2004. "Meetings and Conferences in Data Mining, and Knowledge Discovery." *http://www.Kdnuggets.com/meetings/index.html* (accessed August 23, 2004).

Microsoft Research. 2006. "Facts About Microsoft Research 2006" *http://research. microsoft.com/aboutmsr/presskit/MSResearchFSO . . .* {accessed June 6, 2006).

Mint. 2003. "Knowledge-enabling your business processes." <http://www.mint*solutions.co.uk/pages.asp?p=46*> (accessed December 16, 2003).

Mossberg, Walter S. 2004a. "New Programs Search Hard Disks Really Well But Has Rough Edges." *Wall Street Journal* March 25, 2004, B1.

———. 2004b. "Verizon Devices Use High-Speed Network for Voice, Web, E-Mail." *Wall Street Journal* December 16, 2004, B1.

———. 2004c. "A Primer on Fighting Spyware." *Wall Street Journal* December 29, 2004, D1-D3.

Morris, Tom. 1999. *Philosophy for Dummies* Wiley Publishing, Inc. ISBN 0-7645-5133-1.

Murray, Bill. 2003. "Defense college's CIO course draws feds government wide." *Government Computer News. http://www. gen.com/vol19_no23/26991.html* (accessed December 30, 2003).

Myron, David. 2003. "Salesforce.com is Going Beyond CRM." http://www. destinationcrm.com/articles/default.asp?ArticlsID= (accessed December 23, 2003).

NAPA. 2001. "The Transforming Power of Information Technology: Making the Federal Government an Employer of Choice for IT Employees." *National Academy of Public Administration*. ISBN: 1-57744-090-0.

NDIIPP. 2003. "Program Announcement" *http://www.digitalpreservation.gov/ programannouncement* (accessed November 14, 2003) or *www.fgdc.gov.*

Needleman, Jacob. 2001. "Wendy, Sim, and Other Philosophers: High School and the Love of Wisdom", *Schools with Spirit*. 2001, 90-106.

NEGP. 2002. "National Education Goals Panel." *http://www.negp.gov/* (accessed November 10, 2004).

NLP. 2004. "Natural Language Processing." *http://research.microsoft.com/nlp* (accessed August 24, 2004}.

Nonaka, Ikujiro and Hirotaka Takeuchi. 1995. *The Knowledge Creating Company* New York: The Oxford University Press, 224-226.

NLSR. 2004."What is the Natural Language Software Registry?" *http://registry. dfki.de/info.htm* (accessed October 15, 2004).

OLAP. 2003. "OLAP and OLAP Server Definitions." *http://www.moulton. com/olap/olap.glossary.html* (accessed January 20, 2004).

Open Text's Livelink. 2003. *http://www. google.com/search?hl=en&ie=UTF- 8&oe=UTF-8&* (accessed December 19, 2003).

Overby, Stephanie. 2003. "IT Consolidation." *CIO Magazine* November 15, 2003, 86-94.

——. 2004. "Lost in Translation the Process of Transferring Knowledge." *CIO Magazine* July 15, 2004, 50-56.

Overview. 2004. "Overview." *http://www.ed.gov/fund/landing/ihtml?src=rt* (accessed November 3, 2004).

Pino, Jerry Ortizy. 2003. "Whatever happened to wisdom?" *http://www.cop. com/info/wisdompg.html* (accessed September 26, 2003).

Perkins, Bart. 2003. "The Forgotten Side of Outsourcing." *Computerworld* September 8, 2003, 42.

Press Releases. 2006. Press Releases January 25, 2006 and January 31, 2006, U.S. Senate Committee on Energy & Natural Resources *http://energy.senate. gov/public/index.cfm?GidrSvyopm=Press_Releases.Detail&AndPressRelease_i . . .* (accessed July 19, 2006).

Prusak, Laurence. 2002. "Foreword." *The Complete Idiot's Guide to Knowledge Management*. Madison, Wisconsin: CWL Publishing Enterprises, xv.

QuickFacts. 2000. "State and County QuickFacts." *http://quickfacts,census. gov/qfd/index.html* (accessed June 27, 2004).

Rao, Madanmohan (Ed.). 2003. *Leading with Knowledge: Knowledge Management Practices in Global Infotech Companies*. New Delhi: Tata McGraw-Hill Publishing Company Limited.

Railey,Gary. 2004. "What are Expert Systems" May 22, 2004. *http://www.ghgcorp.com/clips/Expert Systems.html* (accessed September 10, 2,004}.

Rauch-Hindin, Wendy. 1986. *Artificial Intelligence in Business, Science, and Industry* 1986 Englewood Cliffs, NJ: Prentice-Hall, 63-70, 78-82.

Ravitch, Diane. 1993. "Enhancing the Federal Role in Research Education." *The Chronicle of Higher Education* April 7, 1993, A48.

REL 2004. "Regional Educational Laboratories." *http://www.mcrel.org/rel/* (accessed November 3, 2004).

Report. 2003. "The OLAP Report." *http://www.olapreport.com/fasmi.htm* (accessed January 30, 2004).

Ribeiro, John. 2005. "Microsoft Research Aims to Ease Development." Timely Topics TechNews for IT Professionals, ACM TechNews 7, Issue 804:June 15, 2005. *http://www.acm.org/technews/articles/2005-7/0615w.html* (accessed June 15, 2005).

Riley, James. 2004. "ACS pushes own IT 'license.'" http://australianit.news. com.au/articles/0,7204,11106986^16123 (accessed October 21, 2004).

Rosenbloom, Andrew. 2004. "The Blogosphere." *Communications of the ACM*, 47, no. 12, December 2004, 31-53.

Rosenthal, Jack. 2001. "On Language: A chief for every occasion, even a chief chief" *New York Times Magazine* August 26, 2001.

Rumizen, Melissie Clemmons. 2002. *The Complete Idiot's Guide to Knowledge Management*. Madison, Wisconsin: CWL Publishing Enterprises, xvi-xvii, 275-284.

Sager, Ira. 2002. "A No-Noncense Book—With A Few Gaps." *Business Week*, November 18, 2002, 70.

Santosus, Megan and Jon Surmacz n.d. "The ABCs of Knowledge Management." CIO Knowledge Management Research Center. <http:// www.cio.com/research/knowledge/edu/kmabcs.html> (accessed December 5, 2003).

Santosus, Megan. 2003. "In the Know Below the Surface." *http://www.cio.com/knowledge/edit/k060503_tacit.html* (accessed June 20, 2003}.

Scheier, Robert L. 2003. "Regulated Storage." *Computerworld November* 17, 2003, 32-36.

Sixth Generation. 1990-. *http://csepl.phy.ornl.gov/ov/node15.html* (accessed November 21, 2004).

Skyrme, David n.d. "The Learning Organization." *http://www.skyrme.com/insights/3lrnorg.htm* (accessed November 26, 2003).

———. n.d. "KM Basics: An Introduction to Knowledge Management." *http://www.skyrme.com/resource/kmbasics.htm* (accessed December 5, 2003).

———. 2002. "The 3Cs of Knowledge Sharing: Culture, Co-opetition and Commitment." *http://www.skyrme.com/updates/u64_fl.html* (accessed November 26, 2003).

SmartBUY. 2003. "The NSW Government's whole-of-government electronic marketplace." *http://smartbuy.nsw.gov.au* (accessed November 26, 2003).

Spam Laws. 2003. "CAN-SPAM Act of 2003." *http://www.spamlaws.com/federal/108s877.html* (accessed December 5, 2003).

Spielhagen, Frances R. and Bruce S. Cooper. 2005. "The Unkindest Cut" *Education Week* April 13, 2005, 24 no. 31: 61.

Standards. n.d. "National Science Education Standards" *http://www.nap.edu/readingrom/books/uses/html/1.html* (accessed June 8, 2005)

Standard. 1996. "What Is a Standard?" Goals 2000: A Progress Report—Fall 1996. *http://www.ed.gov/G2K/ProgRpt96/standard.html* (accessed November 10, 2004).

Standards-Based Reform. 1998. "Goals 2000: Implementing Standards-Based Reform" *http://www.ed.gov.pubs/G2KReforming/g2ch3.html* (accessed November 10, 2004).

Sternberg, Robert J. 1990. *Wisdom: Its Nature, Origins, and Development.* New York, NY: Cambridge University Press.3-9.

Stewart, Tom. 2002. "The Case Against Knowledge Management." *Business 2.0,* February 2002 *http://www.kmnetwork.com/KnowledgeManagementRealTimeE* (accessed December 5, 2003).

Sutcliffe, Alistair and Nikolay Mehandjiev, Guest Editors 2004. "End-User Development." *Communications of the ACM,* September 2004, 47, no. 9: 31-66.

Symonds, William C. 2004. "No Child: Can It Make The Grade?" *BusinessWeek* March 8, 2004, 78-80.

Tacit K. 2002. "Tacit Knowledge Systems Licenses KnowledgeMail Software to Kodak." *http://www.bizjournals.com/sanfrancisco/stories/2002/04/22/dai* (accessed December 16, 2003).

Tarpy, Cliff. 2003. "67210 Beulah's Boeing." *National Geographic* December 2003, 132-138.

Tomasi, Carlo, Arbas Rafii, and Ilhami Tkorunoglu. 2003. "Full-Size Projection Keyboard for Handheld Devices." *Communications of the ACM,* 46, no. 7: 70-75.

Totty, Michael. 2004. "Making Them Pay." *Wall Street Journal* March 22, 2004, R1-4.

TREC. 2004. "Text Retrieval Conferences (TREC) Overview." *http://trec.nist.gov/overview.html* (accessed August 17, 2004).

Tufte, Edward R. 2001. The Visual Display of Quantitative Information. 2nd ed. 2001. Cheshire, CT: Graphics Press, 40.

Voohis, Dan. 2005. "IBM gift creates new tech courses." *Wichita Eagle* June 27, 2005, 1A.

Webster. 2003a. *Merriam Webster's Collegiate Dictionary,* 11th Edition.

Webster. 2003b. *Webster's New World Computer Dictionary,* 10th Edition.

Willcocks, Leslie, et. al. 2003. "Knowledge in outsourcing—the missed business opportunity." *Knowledge Management News* November 26, 2003. *http://www.kmmagazine.com/xq/asp/sid.364BEE6C-2FFB-4F3* (accessed November 28, 2003).

Willets, Larry G. 1996. "The Chief Learning Officer: New Title for New Times." *http://www.reengineering.com/articles/may96/clo.htm* (accessed November 26, 2003).

Wingfeld, Nick. 2004. "20 Questions." *Wall Street Journal Technology, The Journal Report* December 13, 2004, R1-R4.

Woodard, Colin. 1997. "Panama Hopes to Create a 'City of Knowledge' Where U.S. Forces Once Ran the Canal Zone." *The Chronicle of Higher Education* May 16, 1997, A37-38.

Worthen, Ben. 2006. "China Builds A Better Internet" *CIO Magazine* July 15, 2006, 41-49

WSU. 2003. *http://www.library.wichita.edu/* (accessed March 10, 2004).

Young, Jeffrey R. 2004a. "Next Up for Open Source: Financial Systems." *The Chronicle of Higher Education* September 10, 2004, A30.

____. 2004b. "5 Challenges for Open Source" *Information Technology*, Section B, *The Chronicle of Higher Education* September 24, 2004, B1-B25.

____. 2005. "From Gutenberg to Google." the *The Chronicle of Higher Education,* June 3, 2005, A24-A27.

YRE. 2003. "YRE Statistics" *http://www.nayre.org/statistics.html* (accessed February 2, 2004).

INDEX

explicit knowledge, 38, 40, 47, 74
extranet, 41, 48, 50, 74

F

FASMI, 61
fast analysis of shared multidimensional information. *See* FASMI
Federal Geographic Data Committee, 14
FGDC. *See* Federal Geographic Data Committee
field of medicine, 39
fifth generation, 19
Firestone, Joe, 59, 68
first official census, 14
4GLs, 17, 18, 61, 72
5GL-Doctor Personal Edition, 40
FOCUS, 19
Fountain of Knowledge, A, 21
four Knowledge Development Agency objectives, 67
fourth-generation languages. *See* 4GLs
Frand, 69
full-time, year-round, 79

G

Gartner Inc., 77
Gerstner, Louis V., Jr.
  on information technology industry, 43
  Who Says Elephants Cant Dance?, 42
GILS. *See* Global Information Locator Service
Global Information Locator Service, 13
globalization, 13
Goals 2000, 54
Goetz, Martin, 19
Google, 21
  Desktop Search, 60
    Web site, 60
  library agreements, 78
Gregorian, Vartan, 10, 66, 68

H

Health Insurance Portability and Accountability Act, 16

HIPAA. *See* Health Insurance Portability and Accountability
Hirsch, E. D., 53
home-schooling, 79
Honeywell International, 41
human factors, 32, 42

I

IBM
  changing the culture of, 43, 75
  keeping IBM together, 43
  Linux, 34
  Lotus Development Corporation, 43
  offshoring, 32
  open source training, 71
Idiot's Guide to Knowledge Management The (Rumizen). *See Complete Idiot's Guide to Knowledge Management, The*
IEEE Spectrum, 21
IEEE-CS. *See* Computer Society
IES. *See* Institute of Education Sciences
IKM. *See* individual knowledge management
ILM. *See* information: life-cycle management
individual finance course, 81
individual knowledge management, 59
information, 23
  definition of, 23
  life-cycle management, 16, 76
  resource manager, 27, 28
  usable, 23
information technology
  industry, 43
  profession, 36, 80
information technology outsourcing, 31
Institute of Education Sciences, 55
Intec Engineering, 40
international tecnoparque, 52
intranet, 41, 44, 48, 50, 62, 72, 74
IRM. *See* information: resource manager
IT profession. *See* information technology: profession
ITO. *See* information technology outsourcing